How Anyone Can Start and Manage a Successful Auto Repair Business

How Anyone Can Start and Manage a Successful Auto Repair Business

OWNER'S MANUAL

Alex Dotson

ISBN: 069253704X
ISBN 13: 9780692537046
Library of Congress Control Number: 2015915424
Alex Dotson: Ruckersville, VA

Table of Contents

Summary

The auto repair business is available to all who desire to be successful in this industry. Whether you are a seasoned automotive technician or someone without automotive experience, but have good management skills, you are included in this lucrative business. Every minute detail will be included in this guide. Not to worry, if you don't know the first thing about an automobile or the auto repair business this guide will have step by step instructions on how to move through the process in a quick, efficient and fluid manner.

Ladies are desperately needed in the auto repair industry. In most cases, the ladies would never consider owning an auto repair facility. The intimidation of possibly not understanding automobiles always seems to get in the way. The ladies naturally possess the important skills that are critical to running a business. So, ladies, please lose that intimidation and open an auto repair facility.

As I just mentioned, the lack of technical knowledge of an automobile is not a deterrent. Mechanical knowledge is the responsibility of your shop team leader so your job is to select an effective team leader and not worry about the technical stuff. I will give you detailed guidelines for selecting and retaining an effective shop team and team leader so don't worry about this.

I will also tell you everything you will need to know about the location, the building and the layout of the building. I will share many exact details as to the configuration of the office, shop and even the parking area. Details such as the size, position and location of electrical receptacles and air lines and much, much more will also be included. I leave nothing to chance when it comes to the building, office and shop. I will even tell you how to park customers' vehicles to prevent damage and to, also, allow the manager to assess workload and determine the status of vehicles.

You will also receive valuable tips on dealing with customers and customer related issues. There is a great deal of psychology involved with effective customer relations so I will be sharing those details with you.

In the shop area I have lots of really great techniques that will enhance the management of the workspace for maximum efficiency. I will give you all of those details and more. Efficiency converts into an improved bottom line so you can see how this can make a huge difference in how your business performs.

I will show you how to develop an effective office team, shop team and professional team. The office team will assure the work is scheduled and coordinated properly, the shop team will make sure all of the work is done in an efficient and professional manner and the professional team will make sure all of your financial issues are addressed and taken care of.

I also have a very complete section dedicated to general business practices. It covers things like business structures, creative marketing and advertising, and business resources available to you which will help you fine tune your business.

After reading this guide from cover to cover you will possess all of the necessary knowledge so you can start and manage your own auto repair facility. If you didn't think you had the knowledge and ability to operate a successful auto repair facility, after reading this guide you definitely will! Rest assured, by following my recommendations in this guide, you will be a huge success in the auto repair industry and of this I am 110% certain!

Disclaimer and Statement of Non-Liability

Welcome to the auto repair industry. Due to the extreme demand for auto repair services, the success rate for the auto repair industry is better than businesses in other sectors. That said, there are circumstances that could cause an auto repair facility to fail.

In this guide, I will give you all of the information, and in great detail, that will allow you to be successful beyond your wildest dreams, but the rest is up to YOU. Although I know you will do well, I can make no guarantees as to the end result of your automotive business venture. All businesses come with inherent risks and you must decide if YOU are up for the challenge and then proceed accordingly.

Another consideration when entering the auto repair field is the risk of personal injury to you, your office staff and your technicians. I have given you my recommendations regarding safety related issues. I have, also, given you my recommendation as to the appropriate government agency (OSHA) that is responsible for implementing and enforcing work place safety regulations. To obtain specific answers to safety related issues, you should contact this agency directly. Ultimately, it is your responsibility as the repair shop owner to be aware of, implement and enforce safety procedures. Whatever happens on your watch is your responsibility.

To be sure, the materials contained in this guide are provided for general informational purposes only and do not constitute legal or other professional advice on any subject matter. SuccessAuto1 LLC and/or Alex Dotson do not accept any responsibility for loss, damage or injury which may arise from reliance on information contained in the guide.

Notice: Due to circumstances which are beyond my control, SuccessAuto1 and/or Alex Dotson cannot be held responsible for errors and omissions that may occur in the content of this publication. Since this publication relies heavily on digitally transferred content, formatting and internet issues, to include individual computer performance, can possibly alter text and layout. Please let me know if you happen to notice an issue so I can, if possible, have it corrected. Thank you for your consideration.

How To Use This Guide

How to use this guide: Good question! To be perfectly honest with you, the concept of, "How to Use This Guide" never crossed my mind. In my way of thinking the reader would simply read the material as they would read any other book, or guide, and that would pretty much be it. My editor, on the other hand, had a different take on this concept. Needless to say, I had a little more work on my hands. Once I put my mind to it I realized, since I am very much in to procedure, technique and systematic methods of doing things, the same should apply to this guide.

Now for the procedure, technique and systematic method for using this guide. You will still be required to read this guide from cover to cover, it's just now you will have a plan. I will give you the best way to maneuver through this guide but I'm definitely not going to say it will be easy. This is not casual reading whereby you read through the material and then move on to something else. This requires very strict focus and concentration so when you are reading this guide you must be in a quiet setting with no interruptions.

A technique that works quite well for me is to get up early in the morning when others are sleeping and do your reading. For many individuals the early morning hours are very quiet and tranquil so your senses are positioned to focus on one important topic. Your mind is also rested and ready to accept fresh, new information.

Of course, the "Night Owls" are thinking that will never work. Good news! The same principle applies to the late night hours. All you really want or need is a little peace and quiet so your mind can function at maximum efficiency and without interruption. Two very important accessories will be a fresh notebook and a couple of good, reliable pens so you can take notes along the way.

Another option is to simply tell your family members and loved ones you are trying to concentrate on some important information. Let them know it is essential you learn all of the important details and, as a result, all of their lives will dramatically improve. Trust me, they will understand and appreciate what you are doing. You can tell your kids you are studying for a very big test and you want to pass with flying colors. They will be very impressed by your actions and you will also be setting a great example for them in the process. You would be telling the truth because going into business is one of the largest tests a person can take. It is a test that you must always pass and hopefully, with the help of this guide, will be with Flying Colors!

I hope you are getting the message: using this guide will require your undivided attention, focus and concentration. Anything less and you will not gain the maximum benefit. Remember, *More Knowledge* equals *More Income*!

Now that I have frightened you half to death I have some good news for you. While reading this guide I have periodically injected some of my personal stories so your mind can relax a bit and be somewhat refreshed for the next technical information. It is important to note these stories are packed with valuable information which is a large part of the learning process generated by this guide. In addition, I made an effort to inject a little humor from time to time so you won't think I'm a total "stick in the mud!". I hope this will be helpful.

My very best advice is, *Please Don't Panic*! There is a lot of information in this guide and I would never expect anyone to get it all the first time through. When I am learning something new it quite often takes about three or more passes for the message to finally sink in.

If you have limited automotive or auto repair experience it could very easily take a bit more time to develop the *Big Picture*. This is in no way a reflection of your intelligence: it's just plain and simple new territory which you must conquer and claim in order to be successful in the fast moving and lucrative auto repair industry.

The most important message I would like to convey at this time is: I am absolutely, positively certain you can do this! Now it's time to focus, concentrate and, above all, achieve your very special goal of Starting and Managing Your Own Successful Auto Repair Business!!

Just so you know, I am available for email and/or on-site consultations so please feel free to email me at **alexdotson1@gmail.com**. I'm waiting to hear from you!

A Few Comments from My Really Good Friend and Editor

By Soraya van Asten

I'm not a "shop girl"; I'm more of a horsey country girl, but I've been to plenty of auto repair shops over the years and have a few comments to make to emphasize some of the things Alex has written in this excellent guide.

In years past, auto repair shops used to call to let me know the expected cost of repairs, or if something had changed regarding the needed repair. I really appreciated this courtesy. In more recent years, this courtesy has pretty much disappeared. It would be great for this courtesy, and Good Business practice to return. I, for one, would become a loyal customer. Too many times have I gone to pick up my vehicle only to get the surprising news that there was a problem and that I owe more money than I expected. This was upsetting and unappreciated and left me with a bad feeling about the shop.

One thing I have never experienced with any auto repair shop is having the tech go on a test drive with me: as Alex recommends. What a Fabulous concept this is! I would So Appreciate the opportunity to have the tech hear and feel my concerns with my vehicle.

Here are some other things that would make me, and surely others, a happy and loyal customer who would tell all their friends about how great your auto repair shop is:

- Explain everything related to the repair of my vehicle in courteous detail.
- Call with the cost estimate in a timely manner.
- Call me if anything changes regarding my repair and explain the details; including the likely additional expense, and if my vehicle will still be ready for pick up at the end of the day.
- Tell me, truthfully, that you are doing your best to keep the repair costs reasonable.
- And naturally: do a good job repairing the vehicle.

One detail I have *Really* missed in recent years is the extra finishing touch of my vehicle getting a good bath and vacuuming. You do this and you will *Really Impress* your client!

My biggest "pet peeve" in recent years is getting my vehicle back with grease on my steering wheel, seats, and floor mat. *Pretty Please Be Sure* to cover these with plastic or paper.

Also, if you find something that looks like it's about to go bad, I would like to know about it. I want to be given the opportunity to decide if I want to fix it now or later. I have hauled horses all over the country and the last thing I want to have happen is to breakdown on the road while hauling horses. I have very much appreciated being told when something looked like it was about to wear out or break, so I could get it fixed before a dangerous breakdown with horses in tow. BUT, I have also had some shops try to convince me I needed a big repair only to find out from another shop that there was no need. Please be honest, you will gain lifetime customers with honesty.

On the subject of clean and orderly shops, I have had many a shop, especially for pickups and larger trucks, where the office was next to impossible to find. There were no signs, and I had to work my way around trucks being worked on, with parts all around, and horrible dirty, oily floors with multiple hazards (hoses, barrels, parts) all over the floor too… It's actually amazing I didn't get hurt. And when I finally found the office, it was a mess and filthy too…really awful. But this was the best and most reasonably priced place to get my diesel pickup fixed… Alex's suggestion to have a well-organized, well-lit, clean shop, along with a professional front office with good signage is very excellent advice!

I have a suggestion for when you make your TV commercial: when you are speaking your lines directly into the camera, it's a great idea to have a good friend next to or behind the camera and speak your lines to your friend. This way you will sound and look very natural, *like you are speaking to a good friend!*

And finally, I'd like to say how interesting and fun it was to help Alex with his first guide: *How ANYONE can Start and Manage a Successful Auto Repair Business.* I learned a lot of things about grammar and writing styles that I had either forgotten or just didn't know about. It's been a very educational process. I especially liked the discovery of how the US and Great Britain differ in their handling of punctuations in relation to the use of quotes. I have always found it very difficult to figure out if a quoted sentence, especially when at the end of a sentence, ended the whole sentence or if it's continuing. Having the period or question mark within the quote, when it's not actually part of the quote but part of the whole sentence, makes it confusing to figure out that the next part is a new sentence. And, having a comma within a quote when it relates to the whole sentence and not the quote doesn't work for me either. Maybe part of my problem is that I am of Dutch (Netherlands, aka Holland) decent and have gone to school there as well as the US.

Apparently, some bright person in Great Britain challenged this use of punctuation with quotes (which I read was created back in the old typesetting days to protect the delicate punctuation pieces) and was successful in changing their rules on this subject. Since protecting the delicate typeset machine pieces is no longer an issue, it seems logical to, well, use logic to change this rule and put the comma or period or question mark outside of the quotes when it's not related to the quotation. In my opinion, this makes for much easier reading. I wish the US would also adopt this rule change. In the meantime, I'm going to adopt the Great Britain rule and maybe if enough people in the US do this, then maybe logic will prevail and the rule will be changed in the US at some point.

And finally (for real this time!), with as many times as we both have read over this guide, I hope that we caught everything that needed to be fixed. If there are still some oversights, please know that we put in a lot of effort to get this guide "just right" and at some point a person just has to say "it's done".

I hope you enjoy this guide and benefit from all the excellent advice imparted in it from the many years of Alex's experience.

Alex and Soraya at SuccessAuto1

About the Author

Hi. My name is Alex Dotson. I hope you are having a great and productive day. Well guess what, it's going to get better. Let me tell you a little secret; if you will simply take the time to read this guide from cover to cover and apply the principles shared within, I am positive you will enjoy success in the auto repair industry that you never thought possible. Now, my story:

To the best of my recollection, my very first interest in mechanically related things began with a Briggs and Stratton lawn mower engine. I was four years old. I would watch my father roll this machine out, touch a few things, pull on a cord, and then it would make this loud sound. He would then push the machine across the yard and wherever he went with the machine, while it was making that noise, the grass always looked really nice. I was totally baffled but extremely curious.

One day after he had finished making the grass look nice with this machine I decided I needed to know how that thing worked. The machine was still setting in the yard so I took it upon myself to mosey on over to it and check it out. Before I got there my father yelled out, "Get away from that lawnmower, you'll get hurt!". Well, I did learn one thing: the machine was called a "lawnmower". That was progress but it still didn't tell me the first thing as to how it worked. He could see the curiosity in my eyes so he made me stand back a little ways and let me look under it. That was helpful but it still didn't tell me much. I was interested in that noisy thing setting on top.

One day my father was mowing and all of a sudden the lawn mower started making a rattling sound. Then, within a matter of seconds it made a loud bang and all was quiet. My father started having a conversation with the lawnmower. He said a few words that I had never heard before but I figured he had been saving them for a special occasion. This must have been it! I asked him what happened and he said, "The engine blew up!". Something told me that wasn't good but at least I learned something new. That big hunk of noisy metal on top of the lawnmower was called an "engine".

A couple days later my father came home carrying something large and shiny: a brand new engine. He put the new engine on his workbench and then walked away. I just stood there and looked at it. My imagination was running wild trying to figure out what was inside of that thing. Fairly soon he returned and told me it was time to "swap the engines out". I liked the way that sounded!

Out came these things called "wrenches" that were designed to remove and replace "bolts". I paid attention to every word that came out of my father's mouth. I was learning about engines! It was very exciting! Now it was time to swap out the engine using wrenches to remove bolts. My father placed the lawnmower on the bench and started turning the bolts and before long the old engine had been removed and the new engine was installed. The "engine swap" was complete. I thought: "That wasn't so bad, I could do that". My father put some oil in the engine and some gasoline in the gas tank. Yep, I learned about "oil and gasoline". He touched a few things, pulled on the cord and the noise was back. Nice job!

The old engine was still on the workbench and there were still a few mysteries that had to be solved. I still needed to know how an engine worked. My father was still in the shop doing something else so I decided I couldn't take it anymore. The wrenches were still lying on the workbench next to the old engine so I picked one up. Aww man, did that feel good! From the first time I laid eyes on that Briggs and Stratton engine I made mental notes as to the location of those things that I now know were bolts. Having watched my father, I understood their purpose. I rolled the engine on its side and looked at the bolts again. This time I had to look closely at the bolts and then look at the wrenches to match up the size. I knew they had to be a snug fit or the bolt wouldn't turn. Now, I had the right size wrenches and it was time to remove some bolts. I tugged on the first one, wouldn't budge. Next bolt, wouldn't budge. Third bolt, same thing. Guess it's not so easy after all!

Out of the corner of my eye I could see my father and he was holding a brass hammer. I didn't know what he had in mind but I knew it was going to be good. The wrench was still on the bolt so my father picked up a shop towel and grabbed the wrench with one hand and with the hammer in the other hand, gave the wrench a quick tap and the bolt was loose. Next bolt, same result. Next bolt, same thing. He handed me the hammer and the wrench and said "your turn". I put the wrench on the bolt, gave it a little tap and it was loose. I took the rest of the bolts out and the bottom cover plate was off.

My very first look at what was inside an engine! My father pointed out the "crankshaft" which was black and blue, the broken "connecting rod", and pieces of broken "piston" and broken "camshaft". With the knowledge of loosening bolts I then removed the "cylinder head" and the disassembly was complete. At that point my father explained how the engine rotated and all of the parts worked together. I still couldn't believe that was how an engine worked but my father knew everything so he had to be right.

The next day I woke up with a thought: I knew how the engine came apart but I didn't know how it went back together. My father explained to me the old engine was too damaged to justify repair so that was why he got a new one. Normally, he told me, you would disassemble the engine, clean and inspect the parts and then get new ones. I broke in with: "But wait a minute! How does the engine go back together?". My father said: "That's simple, simply read the book, or manual, and it will tell you everything you will need to know to put it back together". I teared up a little and said, "But I don't know how to read that book". My father said: "Well, your mother has been trying to help with your reading for some time now but you don't want to learn how to read".

I could fix that! So I ran into the house yelling, "Mama, Mama, I want to learn how to read, I want to learn how to read!". Now, you can see the power engines and automobiles had over me. I really didn't like to read but the thought of not being able to work on engines was more than I could deal with. Automobiles and engines have been one of the most powerful forces in my life and will continue to be for the rest of my life.

Needless to say, that was just the beginning. When I was nine years old I had worked on more automobiles, trucks and farm equipment than you could ever imagine. At the ripe old age of twelve I was working on gray market Volkswagens mainly because no one else would touch them. An oil change which included cleaning the strainer was $2.50 and, a tune up and valve adjustment which included parts and labor was $12.50. Based on the prices I guess you can tell I've been doing this for a long, long time.

I could go on forever talking about myself but my primary objective is to give you an idea as to how long I've been in the automotive business. Please believe me when I tell you this is not my first *Rodeo*. Except for a few years in college and a wonderful and exciting four years in the US Navy, I have spent the vast majority of my life in the field of auto repair and auto repair shop ownership.

In the interest of full disclosure I have been a building contractor and real estate broker for a bit over ten years and, as a result, I am in a position to consult with auto repair shop owners to purchase repair facilities or to purchase property on which they can build a new facility. It works quite well because I know exactly what they want and need. A very nice combination.

In the Introduction I mention I was going to bestow thirty five years of automotive experience on my readers. That's not exactly true: it's a lot more, but, since this guide is primarily dedicated to starting and managing an auto repair facility then I will only declare thirty five years as the actual time I have owned and managed an auto repair facility.

I hope as you read through this guide you can see it is clearly not boilerplate information. This is all original information learned the hard way. In all honesty, I can't take full credit for all of the information in this guide but I can take full credit for paying close attention to others, drawing my own conclusions and presenting all of the critical information in such a way that you, the reader, can gain maximum benefit. You will not believe the thrill when you encounter your first business situation and you know the answer as though it was second nature. Now, can you tell I'm excited about this guide?!

To be clear, I am just an average kind of guy with lots of ideas. If you met me on the street you wouldn't know me from anyone else in the crowd. Actually that's not true: I would be the guy with the big smile on his face and walking like a bat-out-of-hell. The point I want to make is this: I am not some huge corporation trying to make a fast buck off of an unsuspecting general public. This guide is the product of many years and many hours of personally getting up early, working late, making a lot of mistakes and then suffering through those mistakes. My primary objective is to keep this from happening to you. My greatest reward will be hearing your success stories.

As previously mentioned, I am available for email and/or on-site consultations so please feel free to email me at **alexdotson1@gmail.com**. I'm waiting to hear from you!

Dedication

Most dedications focus on one or two individuals at the most. In my case I would be negligent if I did not mention the five people who were very instrumental in the creation of this guide. This dedication could very easily be the source of another book but, in the interest of efficiency, I will make it as brief as possible and still give credit where credit is due. Since each of these individuals were essential to the creation of this guide I am going to present them in the order in which they had an influence on and in my life.

The first individuals will be no surprise: my father and mother. They both did an excellent job of shaping my life but with totally different approaches. You see, my mother (the teacher) wanted me to be a doctor, lawyer, or engineer and there was nothing wrong with that. My father was very respectful of my mother's wishes but noticed that, at a very early age, I really enjoyed working on mechanical things and, that I was mesmerized by automobiles. As you may guess, a happy medium was achieved.

I believe in the principle of "ladies first", so I'll start with my mother's point of view. Although I was convinced reading, writing and grammar skills would never have a purpose in my life, my mother knew otherwise. I could not begin to tell you the number of sessions my mother and I had that were dedicated to writing and grammar skills. I guess after all of these years she just may have been doing the right thing. Who am I kidding? Of course she was doing the right thing. She was my mother, she could do no wrong! Long story short, I learned my writing and grammar skills. Now I had the knowledge so someday, I don't know, maybe I could write a book. Funny how life works!

My father was what you would call the great observer. I guess I must have unknowingly learned this valuable trait from him because I am exactly the same way. You see, he could observe any given situation and take away totally different lessons from others who observed the same situation. He was able to pick up on details and nuances that others were unable to detect. This is how I was able to acquire all of the valuable knowledge for this guide.

As I mentioned, because of my father's observation skills he noticed very early on how much I enjoyed all things mechanical. I was curious about machinery but automobiles were a different story. I just couldn't take my mind off of cars. As a kid I can't begin to tell you how many custom cars I designed and built in my mind. I have no idea where all of the details came from but they were all right there and crystal clear.

I have a little story that I just have to tell you. It has to do with my father and a life affirming occurrence he was instrumental in creating for me. I was fifteen years old at the time of this event but, as I mentioned earlier, I had been developing a love for automobiles since age four. My uncle owned an Oldsmobile dealership in a small village about two hours from where we lived. We would go for visits from time to time and while there we would all go to the dealership and look at some of the new cars and chat about various improvements he had made.

During one of our visits my father came over and whispered in my ear and said, "Don't say anything to anybody else but we are going to run down to the dealership and look at a special car". My uncle, my father and I jumped in the car and went to the dealership and there sat a brand spankin' new little red two door coupe. It was an Olds 4-4-2. If you are reading this and you are familiar with the Olds 4-4-2 then I bet you know where this is going. In 1963 they were one of the fastest cars on the road, and now it was time to go for a little test drive. My uncle was in the driver's seat, my father was in the front passenger's seat and I was in the back seat. So, down the road we went with me thinking, this thing really isn't that fast and wondering what the big deal was. We worked our way through town and out to the main road. My uncle pulled out on the main highway and got the car fairly straight in the road and then all hell broke loose. All I could hear was a loud roar which quickly turned to a whistle reminiscent of a jet engine and I was holding on for dear life. It was a sensation I had never felt before in my life. If I thought cars were kind of neat before, I was head over heels in love with them now! From that point on my life was dedicated to automobiles.

Thanks to my father I was presented with the right input and pointed in the right direction so I could spend my life doing exactly what I loved: repairing automobiles and making them go fast. The bottom line: my mother taught me effective writing skills and my father identified my passion. The result was this guide. What a winning combination!

Soraya and Neffy Smiles

Now for the next important event that was crucial to the creation of this guide. In comes my really good friend Soraya. I met her while she was in the process of short-selling the house she lived in. She was somewhat overwhelmed by everything that needed to be done so I decided I would give her a hand. It was a lot of work but we managed to pull it off in a timely manner and the house closed on schedule. Our meeting did come with a high price though; it was due to the death of two close and dear loved ones within five months of each other. This occurrence really knocked her for a loop but she was determined that life must go on. There is a country song with the words, "When life throws you curves, you learn how to swerve". Soraya learned how to swerve.

So, how did Soraya help make this guide happen? Well, without her influence writing this guide would have never crossed my mind. At the time she was a member of a travel and writers group. In other words, you could travel and live anywhere in the world that you wanted and write books to make a living. The originators, Gary and Merri Scott, were planning a three day writer's camp in the little town of West Jefferson, North Carolina, on a Labor Day weekend. The problem was Labor Day was fewer than two days away and we had four days' worth of things to do before we could go. Soraya was a member so there was no out of pocket cost for the seminar. One guest was permitted so, if I wanted to go, I could. To sweeten the deal, Gary and Merri even gave us use of two of their nicest cottages. We had to think of a way to go!

Long story short, we did it. We looked at our To Do list and set our priorities. The most important items we were able to accomplish and the rest we delegated. The seminar was located on a small retreat in a very secluded area so we had to take the old Jeep Cherokee. Down the road we went in the packed out Cherokee with Neffy (a very large and wonderful dog) and Pretty Boy (a silly cat) headed for the seminar. It was a three and a half hour trip that took five hours. It took almost an hour of mountain road travel time to get to the cottages.

The primary purpose of the trip was because Soraya wanted to attend and I was just going along for the ride. After all, on what topic would I write a book? The next day we headed to the seminar, got some good seats close to the front and settled in. The seminar started and I figured if I was here I may as well try to learn something, so I sat up straight and listened. About a half hour went by and I was paying attention but kind of halfheartedly. I was still trying to figure how all of this would apply to me. About that time Gary made a comment that hit me like a ton of bricks. The comment was: "If you have something to say, you have something to sell!". It took about a minute for that thought to sink in and all of a sudden it occurred to me that I did have a lot to say! From that point on I listened to every word that came out of Gary's mouth.

After the seminar I started thinking of all the things I could say something about and was overwhelmed with all of the choices. So, I made the decision to focus on what I knew best: auto repair. I had been living and breathing auto repair for most of my life so what better topic to write about? It occurred to me I was constantly observing all of the auto repair shops that I passed on a daily basis. I always had the urge to go in and ask: "Why don't you clean up that parking lot, get rid of the junk and park those cars more neatly? Oh yeah, paint the building and invest in some good signs. By the way, clean up the shop so it has a nice professional appearance!". These are things I've wanted to say for quite some time now so finally I'm saying it. It's all in this guide.

So, to my Father, Mother, Soraya, and Gary and Merri Scott, thanks a bunch. I couldn't have done it without you!

Soraya and Kapri in Colorado

Very Special Thanks

I want to do an extra special "Thank You" to my really great friend Soraya. If you read the Dedication you will recall she was the source of my inspiration for writing this guide. She was, and still is the driving force for this publication. She has also spent many, many endless hours making sure this publication made it to market in an accurate and timely manner.

Although she was faced with the challenges of caring for her elderly, ailing mother she always managed to find the time to work with me on this project. She is presently living in Ecuador and I am currently back in the states. I have honestly lost track of the number of hours we spent on video phone going over the manuscript, and often, into the very early morning hours. It was a grueling and time consuming process but Soraya stuck with it to completion.

I will have to say, we had our "spirited" but friendly debates related to grammar and punctuation. In my own defense I think I was right once or twice. Well, Soraya may have given me credit for being right once but, "Hey" we got it done and that's all that matters.

So, thanks again Soraya for all of your help. Writing and publishing is very much unrelated to what I am accustomed to doing so your expertise in this area was a true lifesaver.

Note: Soraya is also a stickler for details so she frequently questions issues related to grammar and punctuation. She did discover a very "Old School" punctuation technique that apparently did not evolve into the twenty-first century in the United States.

This is one quite obvious error which has been perpetuating itself for entirely too long. It has to do with the placement of final punctuation in relation to quotation marks. In almost every case you will see the quotation marks outside of the final punctuation: **"example."** This is the standard of the US industry and it is incorrect!!! Great Britain enacted a law in the early 1900's to change this punctuation to accommodate a logical thought process. The United States was apparently not paying attention and, as a result, failed to make the same and appropriate punctuation adjustment. The punctuation should appear as: **"example".** See the difference? This makes sense!!! I could go on for days on this topic but it will not help you succeed in the automotive repair industry so I will stop at that. I will stick to the "logical" method for this and other publications. For more information go to "grammargirl.com" to get all of the history concerning this topic. Very interesting!

Introduction

Okay: this is your big day! This may very well be the first day of the rest of your life. If you have made the final decision the auto repair business is your ultimate goal and way of life then you have definitely come to the right place. You will find, this auto repair shop owner's guide will provide you with very specific step by step instructions on how to start and manage a successful auto repair facility. I will provide you with every detail so you will never have to guess or wonder what to do in any given situation. Whether you are new to auto repair or a seasoned professional, you will find plenty to learn from this guide.

Let's say you have been working for someone else for some years now and your lifetime dream has always been owning your own successful auto repair business. This guide is definitely your ticket to success. Maybe you are a fantastic auto mechanic who can repair any car that has rolled across the face of the earth but lack the knowledge and experience to start and manage a business. With labor rates well over $80 per hour and part sales with 50-100% markup it's easy to see the profit potential. You are a seasoned professional who deserves to be rewarded for your expertise. As automobiles get more complex there are fewer people with the ability to learn and retain the necessary information to diagnose and correct issues with these marvels of technology. As a result, competition is reduced and, with fewer automotive facilities, demand for your services will increase.

Although this guide addresses starting an auto repair facility, it also includes the ongoing management principles for a successful auto repair facility. For this reason it is very important that I address the needs of all those hardworking individuals who are already in the business of diagnosing and repairing automobiles. I can tell you as a matter of fact I am very good at some things but not very good at others and I accept that as a reality. The same applies to you. You could be a fantastic technician who can easily diagnose and repair automobiles in your sleep but may not have been exposed to all of the details required to operate a profitable auto repair facility. In this case, this guide is for you!

Here is another scenario. Let's say you've never worked on an automobile in your life and you think starting your own auto repair shop is out of the question. Well, guess again! In this case, if you consider yourself a good business manager then this guide will supply you with all of the knowledge you will need to start and operate a very successful automotive repair facility. There are many critically important details that must be implemented in order to achieve this success and they are all contained in this guide. If you read this guide from start to finish and follow my advice your automotive business will thrive.

Ladies, Ladies, Ladies! You are a very important part of this process. It may or may not have occurred to you but the ladies are also perfectly capable of starting and operating a successful auto repair facility. At this time I will go a step further: the ladies are, in most cases, the best business managers. Ladies are excellent communicators, efficient organizers and are really great multi-taskers. These are extremely important traits that are quite necessary in the operation of a successful auto repair facility. You may or may not know all of the intricate details as to how an automobile functions but that is not an issue. I will give you all of the necessary details for acquiring an effective shop team leader and shop team. Their task will be to take care of all of the technical automotive details so you will be free to make sure the business runs smoothly. *ALL* of the necessary details are included in this guide so, not to worry, you will do great!

I bet you have been thinking about starting your own auto repair facility for some time now and, as a result, you have also been checking out your future competition to see how they are doing. As you evaluate each operation you are thinking to yourself, "I can do better than that!" and you would be right. You look at these repair shops and start to critique them. The building doesn't look very nice, there are cars sitting everywhere and in disarray, there's junk lying around, and if you were a customer you couldn't even figure out how to get into the building. You've done your research so you know the owner is making a decent living. You rationalize, if this person is making a living then you could be very successful and, once again, you would be right. Organization, knowledge and good management practices are the key to creating a profitable and thriving automotive repair business.

This said, get ready for the adventure of your life because I am about to bestow upon you 35 years of automotive business knowledge and experience that cannot be found in any other class, publication, or report you can find anywhere else. I had to learn this stuff the hard way! As you might guess, the "hard way" can be very time consuming and extremely costly so you will be spared this phase of the process. The concepts and principles which will be presented to you in this guide are the result of many hours of hard work, agonizing mistakes and many problem solving sessions. I am not going to ask you to do anything difficult or unreasonable but it will require strict personal discipline and an unwavering attention to detail. Success is available to all, and of course, that includes you! You owe it to yourself and your family to pursue your dreams and become a successful, contributing member in your community. You will, most certainly, enjoy the respect and admiration from all those who associate with you.

Alex and Soraya at ZipQuest in Fayetteville, NC

My Story

When I think of all the things that happened to me in the process of starting and running my automotive repair business I often wonder how I survived. I knew how to work on cars but didn't have a clue as to how a business operated. I was fairly sure all I had to do was charge the customer for labor and materials and I was good to go. But wait, I needed customers to make that concept work. I could fix that problem: all I had to do was advertise and people would come flooding in. Much to my disappointment that flood of customers was, in reality, more like a drip and as you may guess, that was a huge problem. I was very impatient so I was determined to make things happen and soon. This is the story of my adventure starting and growing my successful auto repair business.

After making the decision to start my business, I worked out all of the details in my mind: my shop would be perfect. It would have multiple lifts, state of the art diagnostic equipment and the latest in alignment tools and equipment. Step number one was to make a list of everything I would need and then simply price it out. Fairly straight forward: what's the problem? I'll tell you what the problem was, the equipment cost $100,000 and I had $15,000. Well, that was the end of my automotive business. I went back to the dealership repair shop and the daily grind.

I still wanted to open my own shop eventually so I decided, instead, to go to work at an independent garage to see how a non-dealer repair shop operated. I was getting a little more excited because, after working exclusively at new car dealerships, I felt like this was progress. The first day I went into work everybody was very friendly and it looked like there was plenty of business, so I decided this arrangement was going to work. The dealerships where I had previously worked were so large and impersonal the customer was just a number that eventually showed up on the bottom line of a profit and loss statement. I wasn't crazy about that concept, so something had to change. Now, finally, I was working at a place where the customer mattered. It was a family owned business so the owners, mechanics and their families all knew each other and frequently socialized. This was the place! At this point I truly appreciated the competitive advantage of a privately owned independent auto repair facility. The dealerships did not stand a chance against this type of operation. This shop had been established for quite some time so, I thought they had it all figured out. I was going to learn how to run my own auto shop: Wahoo!

I was always aware of how the dealerships managed and organized their service areas and was careful to take notes. I evaluated everything they did and decided which techniques were great ideas and which techniques were not so great. I took the *not so great ideas* and decided that certain features were good so I combined the good characteristics and *created a great idea*. Now it was time to see how an independent facility operated which would help supply me with the final missing links I needed to start my own business.

At the end of the first day of work at the independent repair shop I came to the startling conclusion; this place was grossly under-equipped, poorly managed and extremely disorganized. My first thought was, "Oh my, what have I done?". Since I was working on commission, I had to at least make a living, not to mention the fact I needed to earn extra money to save and equip my own shop. I thought maybe I was simply over reacting and everything would be okay. I decided to adopt a positive attitude toward this situation and move forward. I also realized they were not going to teach me anything about the operation of an independent auto repair facility but I was still going to make this a learning opportunity. Even though it may not be nice to say: learning from the mistakes of others is very cost effective because they are the ones who suffer the loss and, if you pay attention, you reap the benefit. I guess you could say this is the basis for this auto repair shop guide. Simply stated, I observed or made all of the mistakes so you won't have to.

Let the learning experience begin! The shop was fairly large with extremely high ceilings and had only one door in and one door out. In order to get a car on a lift it was necessary to come in the front overhead door, make a sharp right turn, go forward and then backward about three times and then finally on the lift. Whew! What a pain! Now it was time to set the lift. For some odd reason all three lifts were only about a foot apart so setup was very difficult. It took fifteen or twenty minutes just to get the car on the lift and set it up. Then, it was time to take the car apart and figure out what was wrong with it. Once I located the problem, all I had to do was write my findings down and submit them to the shop owner to get authorization. Simple enough! Well, you would think so. The first thing he asked was, "Are you sure?". I responded, "Of course I'm sure!", at which time the owner decided to come out and double check my diagnosis. Not a problem, good quality control is very important. An extra set of eyes almost always helps: just not this time. I was very confident with my diagnosis but the non-mechanic owner had different ideas. Long story short, I compromised my position in an attempt to keep the job moving. It didn't help! By now almost forty minutes had passed and I hadn't even begun a repair on this vehicle. I'm thinking, "I'm on straight commission, man I'm making the big bucks now!".

Another thirty minutes went by and no answer. I went into the office for the third time to inquire as to the status of the job. The owner's response was: "I don't have time to call the customer now; take the car out and bring in another one". Crap! It's been almost two hours and now I have to put it back together and take it out. Oh no!!! Remember the one door in, one door out? The door out was now blocked! This was getting ridiculous. How does this guy plan on making any money?!

Do you see where this is going? Nowhere! This was a daily occurrence and not just for me but all of the technicians. Want to hear something funny? This guy was actually making a living doing this! How you ask? Because there are so few qualified people out there to compete for all of the auto repair work that it's almost impossible to fail!! For sure, you won't be making much money but at least you will still be open for business. Imagine the profits you could earn if you had a well-managed operation.

I stayed at this shop for another six months and finally decided, enough was enough. Once again, I thought about opening my own shop and this time with renewed energy. If this guy could make a living, I could make a killing. I knew every detail as to how I would run my shop. I decided, since I could not acquire all of the tools and equipment I wanted, I would have to start with the basics and work my way up from there. I knew the importance of accurate diagnosis of problems and the quick and efficient repair of those problems so good equipment was essential. Now, I made a new list of tools and equipment. This list was in no way as extensive as my first list but it was sufficient to offer quality, cost effective repairs to my customers. The out of pocket cost was far less than I had estimated on my first attempt to start my business. Originally I had figured almost $100,000 and now it was a mere $10,000! That was a number I could live with. Due to lease/purchase opportunities and some really great deals I was actually able to acquire more and better equipment than I ever thought possible. I was on my way!

Now I needed a building. I recalled the old real estate concept of "Location, Location, Location" and I figured that was a very important detail. Time to get serious: this was going to be a commitment that was going to cost me money and, with a five year lease, I was going to be obligated for some years to come. At this point there was no turning back. In the past I had chickened out, so I had to ask myself, "Am I in or am I out?". This time the decision was much easier: I was not turning back! I had my fill of dealerships and poorly managed independent shops so I was definitely IN!

I set out to do some market research and determine my location. I knew the area very well so I had certain target areas. Of course, I wanted a good customer base so, traffic volume was important. I tried to avoid heavily congested areas because customers may experience difficulty with access and I didn't want that! Off I went on my mission. I figured, in the interest of efficiency, I would try to locate close to where I lived so I started cruising around making observations and taking notes. I found some interesting possibilities but felt more investigation was in order. Since location was very important, it was worth the extra time and effort to get this right. I studied my notes and set off again. My phase two search was fruitful because I discovered some very good possibilities. I made the phone calls and carefully noted details of each location. Everything looked good so, now, all I had to do was make my selection and sign on the dotted line.

Because of my work schedule and doing my own leg work to start my business, a week had passed and I had not been able to get back with anyone on any of the possible locations to get a lease agreement to read and sign. The weekend had arrived so it was time to take it easy after a very hectic week and relax. My wife and I decided it would be nice to do something different and range out a little.

Some friends had recently opened a new restaurant and we were invited as their special guests so we figured that would be a nice treat for a Saturday night. We hopped in the car and headed to the restaurant. It was fairly close to the house but it was in one of our larger shopping malls and tended to be very congested. As a result, we tried to avoid the area whenever possible. Our friends; however, saw it as a really great location for their business and made the commitment.

When we went into the restaurant it was completely full. The owners were extremely good friends of ours so they had held a table for us and we were given the VIP treatment. As we were waiting for our food, I wondered how they could be so busy on their opening night. They had done minimal advertising because the idea was to make sure everything worked as designed and then have their grand opening event but the place was totally packed out. Oh yes, they were busy because of Location, Location, Location. Where have we heard that before? I thought to myself, this area would work for me but it's just too congested so that would never work. I told myself to forget about it. We enjoyed our meal, thanked our friends for the invite and headed home.

As we pulled out of the parking lot we got on to the "ring" road that circled the mall and realized traffic was much lighter. As we were driving around the mall my wife looked up and said, "Look, there is a vacant automotive shop!". Sure enough, it was: WOW!! We stopped briefly to check it out and then talked about it on the way home and decided the rent would be too high which might make it hard to realize a decent profit. But, even though it was a congested area the access was very easy, so I rationalized this location could be worth the extra cost. I decided to check into it because, you never know, it could work! I revisited the site and there was no contact information. The building needed some maintenance and it looked like it was full of junk. I thought, if I could work a deal with the owner, I may be able to get a break on the rent.

Without any way of getting in touch with the owner, I started asking adjoining property owners if they knew who owned the property and I quickly got all of the contact information I needed. In addition to the contact information, I also got the inside scoop as to what was going on with the property. The owners had problems with a previous tenant who had vacated under the cover of darkness and had stuck them with three months past due rent. Apparently they took off so fast they left everything behind. The owners had obtained prices for cleanup but decided it was going to cost too much so renting the building was out of the question: at least for now.

I decided if, all they needed was to empty the building, I could do that. I figured if they would allow me a month's rent, I could clean it out and be ready to open by the end of the month. The rental amount had never been discussed so I figured I should talk to the owner and nail that amount down. He told me the rent had been $950.00 and said he would like to continue getting that amount. I asked him about how much he would allow me on rent if I did the cleanup. He was very excited about that idea because there was no out of pocket expense for him, not to mention he wasn't getting rent anyway so had nothing to lose. Finally I was making some headway. Knowing he was very motivated, I posed the question: "What would you allow me on rent?". He thought for a minute and said, "How about three months?". Now remember, I was prepared to do it for one month's rent so I jumped on it. I signed the lease and I was in! To sweeten the deal there was no security deposit required. Could it get any better? Well, I'm not done yet!

I did it: I now had my shop. The next day I got the keys. Time to go to work and deliver on the promises I had made to myself and to others. I will admit for the first time, I was a little nervous. Reality had set in. I took this as a positive since the pressure and the nervous energy would help me perform and accomplish my mission.

First, I had to figure out what the heck I had gotten myself into. I opened the walk-in door: I couldn't get in. I opened one of the overhead doors: couldn't get in. The next door and then the next: couldn't get in. Oh no, I was in over my head in more ways than one! What was I going to do? Only one thing I could do: start dragging things into the parking lot and sort. I started grabbing and tossing. Mostly carpet at first, then I found a new car stereo still in the box. That was encouraging. I kept digging and pulling stuff out and then I hit gold. In the midst of all of this stuff; mostly new stuff, and some old stuff, were enough materials and supplies to outfit at least five custom vans. There were complete cabinet sets, captain's seats, speakers, interior panels, custom lighting, and much more, all new and still in the box. It finally set in, I was going to come out of this smelling like a rose. I couldn't believe my luck!

Now it was time to sell! Here I thought I was going into the automotive repair business but now I was in the business of selling custom van accessories: at least for the time being. The original plan was to haul everything away to the landfill but now I would be able to make money off of this stuff. I had a really great location so I was sure everything would sell fine. At the time there was no Craigslist so I had to rely on the local Trading Post and newspaper. The delay in advertising would cost me several extra days before I could start selling the building contents. I was very impatient and, at the same time, very concerned about how well and quickly this stuff would sell. Time would tell.

At the same time, I was anxious to get my auto repair business up and running. I had a lot on my mind and was hoping for the best. The ads came out on a Friday which meant that would be the BIG day. I got up early that morning in anticipation of droves of people showing up and buying everything. Eight o'clock came and I was ready: Nobody! Nine o'clock - Nobody! This wasn't looking good. I started to panic: what was I going to do if I got stuck with all of this stuff? Finally someone showed up around ten o'clock. They looked around, bought a few things and left. Well, at least that was a start. Several more people showed and bought a few things. I thought, I shouldn't complain, it's better than nothing but this process is going to take forever, and I didn't have forever. The day continued on and I sold more items but still had a long way to go before I got rid of everything. I figured it was a Friday so what did I expect. With Saturday coming up, sales would be much better. I decided to call it a day so I locked up and went home. I was positive tomorrow would be a better day. The excitement was waning but I was still optimistic.

Saturday morning came and I was ready to go so I headed to the shop to get ready for the crowd. I was right, the people showed up in numbers and were buying. Finally my plan was back on track. The items were leaving but, unfortunately, it was clear everything would not sell that weekend. At least eighty percent had to sell before I would have enough room in the shop to start setting up the shop for my repair business. More delays that I really didn't have the patience for. Something had to happen and quick!

I thought to myself: "I wish someone would just come in and buy all this stuff!". No sooner than that thought came to mind, a gentleman drove up, got out of his car and started looking around. He was there for about twenty minutes looking at everything at least four or five times. Finally he came over to me and asked, "So how much will you take for everything you have here?". I tried to not look startled but it wasn't easy to keep a "poker face" and stay calm and cool because this was my big chance to make everything go away. I didn't know what to say. Numbers were running through my head and out of nowhere I blurted out "five thousand!". As soon as I said it I thought to myself, "Well that's the end of that deal". The gentlemen stood there for about thirty seconds looking at the items and then looked at me and said, "OK, you've got a deal!". I thought to myself, "What just happened here?". Whatever it was, it definitely worked for me! I could feel the excitement in the air! Finally I could get started with my automotive business.

Bright and early the following Monday morning my purchaser showed up with a moving truck and two helpers and within about an hour and a half I had a completely empty shop: cleaned to the walls. Now I could retrieve all of the tools and equipment I had purchased, including my hand tools, from the various locations and get them into the shop. It was time to go into business!

The building was already set up for auto repair so it was not difficult to arrange the equipment and hand tools. Most of the time was spent on cleaning and painting. A clean, bright, well-organized work area was very important to me so I felt it was worth the additional effort. Also, I felt customers would be impressed by the appearance and organization of the work area and, therefore, it would boost business. The configuration of the shop meant customers would have a clear view of the work area so neatness was very important.

All of this took about a week and I felt that was a reasonable amount of time. I started to relax a bit knowing opening day would be soon! A few more details and I would be done. All I had left to do was install my shop sign, get my business license, do some Grand Opening ads, and I was open for business.

About a week and a half had passed since the building had been cleared out so I felt really good about my progress. I was sure as soon as the ads came out and the banners went up that within about a week or two, at the most, I would be busy. I didn't see how I could miss. Well, opening day came and went and not a single customer! The next day came and went, still no customers. This was very confusing: didn't these people know I would do a great job at a fair price? Why would they go anywhere else? My ads were very clear as to the kind of work I would do and how efficient and cost effective I would be so I couldn't figure out what the problem was.

Two more days went by and nothing was happening. I passed the time by walking around the shop wiping down the equipment and organizing my tool box. Finally, I got tired of this activity and decided to go over and sit on one of the workbenches to think about what was going on and what I was going to do about it. As I sat there thinking and listening to the radio, the news came on and what I heard almost took my breath away. The top story went like this: "Folks, it's official, we are in a recession". I guess I wasn't paying attention because I didn't realize anything was wrong with the economy. I sat there motionless for what seemed like an hour. I was almost to the point of tears. I said to myself, "Man, you really did it this time!!". In my mind I had put myself in a jam that was going to be difficult to get out of. What was I going to do? Then I started suffering from PMS, you know, "Poor Me Syndrome". That lasted for about fifteen minutes or so and then all "Hell" flew into me. That's when I decided I wasn't going down that easily!

So, this is what I did: I was located next to a large shopping mall with many thousands of cars coming and going each day. All I needed to do was give them a reason to drive across the street and come into my shop. If I got one tenth of one percent of all the cars that came through that mall parking lot I would have so much business I wouldn't be able to stand it. What would be quick, simple and inexpensive that would yield quick results? This was a demanding request but I was in a big hurry. I could walk up to people and talk to them and see if I could convince them to bring their cars to me but I was afraid they would be startled or frightened by being approached in a mall parking lot, so that would not work.

The only other choice I felt I had was to place flyers on the windshields of cars. I had a bunch printed up in bright yellow figuring they would be easy to see. I stuck them under the wiper blades of the parked cars as quickly as I could so I could get back to the shop and wait for the customers to show up. I got about half of the flyers handed out when mall security came by and informed me that placing flyers on car windshields was prohibited and I had to stop immediately!

I still had a hand full of flyers and I wanted to get them into the hands of potential customers so I went into the mall and started handing them out. I stopped at a small clothing store and asked the lady if I could leave a few flyers for her customers and she said I could. As I was leaving she made a comment that caught my attention. Her comment and observation unlocked one of the secrets to my success! Her comment was to the effect: a number of people wanted to bring their cars to me but didn't think I was open because they had not seen any cars in or around the building.

Okay, time to think fast: what could I do to get vehicles in and around the building? I had an idea so I ran back to the shop as quickly as I could and started calling all of my friends. The deal I made was this: bring every car you can spare to the shop and I will work on them for free and you only pay for the parts! Within two days the shop and parking lot was full and the rest was history. Within a week the shop was full of paying customers. Finally, I was on my way to success!!

I have been telling you my story because I wanted to make it very clear starting an automotive business is not always a bed of roses. To be sure, this is only a small part of my story but I think you get the idea. Your story will be different since every business is unique and will present you with many different challenges. Just remember to face every challenge with a positive mental attitude and the belief that everything will be "all right". Keep an open mind, be solution conscious and any obstacles you may encounter will be easily resolved. Success will be yours!

Women in the Automotive Repair Industry

I must be perfectly honest with you when I started this guide (and without giving the subject much thought) my focus was on male automotive technicians who, much like myself way back when, desperately want to open their own auto repair facilities. I guess I wasn't thinking clearly when I mentally omitted the ladies from this lucrative industry. To explain this "wake up call", I'd like to reintroduce my very excellent friend Soraya (read more about her in the "Dedication") who is actually the driving force behind this guide. You see, in the early stages of this guide, she did my proofreading (and still does).

As Soraya would read through what I had written, she had many questions about what certain terms meant. I would always respond with: "The guys in the automotive business understand what this means, so those extra details are just not very important". Well, I guess I used that answer one time too many. Needless to say, I received a lecture I won't be forgetting for a long, long time. I will spare you the exact details but the essential message was, "Women were perfectly capable of successfully operating any kind of business and that includes auto repair, but they must have all of the details in order to do so". Now ladies and guys, here is a brief little quiz. Did I agree with her or did I disagree with her? And the correct answer is, Yes, I did agree with her! I agreed primarily because she was absolutely spot-on correct and, secondarily, because I'm a lot of things but I'm no dummy: Friendship must prevail!

No more assumptions on my part! From here on out there will be plenty of detailed facts, information and my most useful personal experiences. Everything in this guide is based on the concept of the best business practices in addition to everything I learned the hard way. Even if you have very little knowledge of how an automobile functions, you will be perfectly competent and capable of owning and operating a successful auto repair facility. I am telling you this because I don't want anyone, and specifically the ladies, to be intimidated by the auto repair business. This industry definitely needs many more individuals with high quality business management skills so please take this information and run with it. The sooner you start the better. My best recommendation is to put your blinders on and focus on your dreams.

Once Soraya enlightened me on the benefits of women in the automotive industry, it really got me thinking. I started recalling all of the situations when I encountered women who were, in some way, affiliated with auto repair. Once I put my mind to it, it occurred to me the ladies were everywhere. I apologize for not noticing: I guess it's just a guy thing! I know when I attended our area automotive aftermarket association meetings (an excellent organization that I strongly recommend joining) I did notice a lot of ladies in attendance with their husbands or significant others but, I guess I figured it was only a social event for them. In many cases the guys, with big smiles on their faces, would introduce their wife or lady friend by giving their name and then include, "and she's also the Boss". Now that I think about it, they really were not kidding. The comment was made in humor but, at the same time, it was the absolute truth. In any case, these couples appeared to get along wonderfully so apparently this arrangement worked for them. The wife or lady friend was running the show up front allowing him to concentrate on repairing customers' vehicles in the shop. I must say, I have noticed the few automotive repair operations with a lady or ladies at the helm definitely displayed characteristics of very desirable management practices. My personal observation was they were all happy and quite successful. For the record, happy and successful is a very nice combination!

Ladies: this information is for your ears only, so please pay close attention to what I'm about to say. To make myself very clear: *you do not have to be in a personal relationship with anyone, including an automotive technician, in order to be successful in the auto repair business.* After all, this is the twenty first century, so the times "they are a-changin' " and to succeed we must also change. These days' women often choose career in addition to family and relationships and there is nothing wrong with that. Although a relationship is an option, I hope you ladies are getting my message of: "*No Relationship Required*" if your desire is to own an auto repair business. After all, this *IS* business!! I want to be loud and clear with this message because your services are desperately needed in this industry. Everything you will need to know about operating a lucrative auto repair business will be covered in detail in this guide and, if you so desire, you will be able to remain independent *And* have your own successful auto repair facility. Keep in mind, for a well-managed auto repair facility, there is a *Lot* of *Money* to be made!

I'm sure many ladies have considered the option of starting their own auto repair facility but were fairly certain this dream was unattainable. I hope to change this trend and soon. One of my primary goals with this guide is to get more ladies into auto repair so I'm counting on you to help me accomplish this task. You have as much right as anyone to make money in this profitable industry so, ladies, please join me in saying: "Be gone with intimidation; I can do this!".

I have placed my contact information at various locations throughout this guide but I want to make absolutely certain the ladies have a resource to call on if they have any questions or concerns regarding the operation of an auto repair facility.

I am available for email and/or on-site consultations so please feel free to contact me at **alexdotson1@gmail.com**. I'm waiting to hear from you!

Ladies and Guys New to Auto Repair

If you are new to auto repair I think it would be a safe assumption you may have very little knowledge of the inner workings of modern day automobiles. If this is the case your primary function will most likely be managing the business. I am willing to bet the big question you now have is: "How is the work I will be charging for going to get done?". It's easier than you may think! This would require a professional shop team and, Yes, you are covered.

In this guide I explain in great detail how to acquire a professional shop team, so not to worry: it will not be that difficult. When a candidate applies for a position all you will have to do is make certain observations, ask the right questions and absolutely verify references and experience. "Due diligence" is key to selecting and building a winning shop team. All of the details are in this guide but here is some advanced information specifically for all those individuals who may be new to auto repair.

There are several business arrangements that can be used to resolve the issue of; "How is the work I will be charging for going to get done?". But, before we talk about business arrangements, I would like to discuss two very important details.

First, if you have limited knowledge of auto repair, you *Must* locate the most highly skilled, highly qualified automotive technician you can get your hands on to be your shop team leader. In addition to their automotive qualifications, it is most important they are someone you can trust to watch your back under any and all conditions.

Second, and equally important: you must be compatible with this person! You will be working with this individual on a daily basis while, at the same time, encountering periodic stressful situations. This can bring out the worst in everyone. You will both have to be patient, behave in a mature manner and perform as a team. You see, the sticking point here is if your shop team leader decides to quit and you are unable to repair vehicles, you have a big, big problem on your hands. This can never happen! But, once again, not to worry: I have a solution for this.

Now let's concentrate on business arrangements which will resolve this issue. My initial inclination would be to suggest forming a Limited Liability Company (LLC), sometimes referred to as a Limited Liability Corporation, with your team leader but that would be a bit hasty. To make this point quite clear, *your auto repair business will operate as an LLC from **Day One***, it's just your shop team leader will not be included at that time. I just discussed the importance of compatibility between you and your team leader so this may take a while to determine. An LLC is a long term commitment which involves some expense so I would recommend delaying this arrangement until you are certain. After all, this is your business so it would be nice if you had complete control over it: at least in the beginning. You'll find more on business structures later in this guide which will help you make this judgment call.

With that said, this is what I would suggest: write up a basic but detailed agreement that covers things like performance expectations, behavior and the importance of following your shop management guidelines. Just so you know, these guidelines are detailed in the shop management section of this publication.

Keep in mind, your shop team leader will also require some concessions if you expect them to sign an agreement of this type. As with your shop team leader, you must also give assurances as to your performance and behavior. An important detail that must be made quite clear is the amount of notice one will give the other should the decision be made to part company. As the owner, it would be wise to state a time frame but also include the statement, "Until a suitable replacement has been secured". In addition, there must be some monetary penalty if either party does not abide by this agreement. At this point all that is required is to date and sign and you have an agreement. If this process makes you nervous then I would definitely recommend consulting an attorney. A word to the wise: please don't complicate this process. If you do, you will never get started in business because you will never be able to acquire a shop team leader.

Once you've been in business for six months to a year, things are moving forward, and your shop team leader is working out as planned, it's time to move to the next level. Now is the time to consider including your team leader in the LLC. Your current shop team leader may or may not be the one you started with and that's OK. As we all know, things can change. One thing to keep in mind is a business relationship is much like a personal relationship: if you are not one hundred percent sure in your heart and in your mind that it's right, *Then Stop!* Your business and its daily operations must be very fluid requiring you and your shop team leader to work in perfect harmony. You will be entering into an agreement (LLC) that will be in effect for many years to come so no rookie mistakes are allowed here!

Of course, you may simply want to continue with the original contract agreement and not include your team leader in your LLC. Some people prefer to have complete control over their business so this would be a business decision on your part. Not to belabor this subject, but if you don't have that "warm fuzzy" feeling about the person who you are in business with then now is really not the time to form a permanent agreement anyway.

However, there are some benefits to including your shop team leader in the LLC. You see, the first logical thought that pops into a business person's head is: "If I include another person in the business that would cut my earnings in half". Nothing could be further from the truth! With the right person, your earnings could easily double and that's a fact. Allow me to explain the theory behind this concept. If you think about it, the idea is very simple.

You, the owner, will be managing the office, making sure every detail is attended to and you will also be doing everything you can to keep your customers happy and returning to your place of business. Remember these are two of your primary objectives; (1) happy customers and (2) repeat business. The reason you will be doing this is because it's your business; you have a vested interest in the business and you have that burning desire to succeed. Okay: hold this thought for a minute.

Here's the deal: you have excellent management skills but, in many cases, don't have the necessary mechanical or technical skills to properly guide your shop team for maximum efficiency. Wouldn't it be nice if you had a shop team leader with a vested interest in the business who also had that same burning desire to succeed as you do? I think everyone will agree this would be a winning combination. Together you would be knocking the ball out of the park and would be doing it on a regular basis! For all of the non-sports fans, this means you will be making (much) more money. To be clear, I'm only joking about the comment concerning non-sports fans but I'm definitely not joking about making more money.

So, to summarize: Make sure you find the most qualified technician available for your shop team leader and then, form a binding agreement which addresses all of the important issues regarding the business. Your shop team leader must also be a reliable, trustworthy individual who you are certain will watch your back under all conditions. Since a business relationship is much like a personal relationship, you must be compatible with this person. There will be stressful situations that will require both you and your shop team leader to behave in a mature, professional manner. Your customers will judge you on this behavior so pay close attention to this detail. If you focus on teamwork you will be amazed as to how efficiently your automotive business will function.

I hope you are picking up on the underlying theme in this guide concerning the importance of teamwork (specifically) and working together (in general). This can very easily be a "make or break" issue for any business. All aspects of your business must work in harmony and your human resources must top this very important list of priorities. Without team work, all you will have is a bunch of people running around in circles bumping into each other. I have personally observed businesses, in way too many cases, where the staff members were running in circles and, yes, I actually witnessed them bumping into each other! I can assure you it was not a pretty sight. Please, by all means, pay close attention to the information in this guide so this scenario never happens to you!

Once again, I am available at **alexdotson1@gmail.com**. Talk soon!

SECTION 1

Let's Get Started!

You are about to be exposed to more critical information than you ever thought possible so how this information is presented is very important. The information in this guide will be presented, for the most part, from the customer's point of view. The reason is, the customer is the basis of all business success and must never be ignored. I will include many tips that will improve customer relations immensely. These tips may appear to be insignificant but you must trust me when I say, they will be the most important information you will get from this guide. These tips will also have customers continuing to come back even though something may have gone wrong on one of the visits to your shop. Customers will forgive and forget and even recommend you to others. Hard to believe but it's true! Once you have acquired their confidence they will be loyal to you through thick and thin. Keep in mind, your best business is repeat business because it doesn't require an advertising expense. It does require effort and time on your part but the return will be well worth it. As long as you treat your customers fairly and honestly they will not bother to shop around for a lower price or try to haggle with you.

All of my concepts will allow you to have a full appointment book and a consistent workload day after day, month after month and year after year. You will be able to charge market rate or more which will allow for a very nice bottom line for your business. I think you will agree with me when I say, this is quite the win-win situation where everybody comes out on top! Making a profit is very important but fairness and honesty should be one of your primary goals. Having a successful business with happy customers is one of the most rewarding experiences you can have in your life.

If you follow as few as half of my concepts you will be enjoying success sooner than you ever imagined. Honestly, if you use all of my ideas you may not be able to handle the workload. I am not trying to discourage you from implementing all of the ideas in this guide; rather, I think it is important you be aware your expansion plans may come sooner than you think. What I am trying to say is: before you start your business make sure you have an expansion plan in place. Under no circumstances are you to waste a second of your time wondering if you will fail. You will succeed and I am a hundred and ten percent confident you will!

I just mentioned if you followed as few as half of the principles and concepts in this guide you will enjoy a level of success you never thought possible. In addition, this success will be realized much sooner than you ever imagined. If for any reason you are unable to implement all of the concepts in this guide, the following information would be highly recommend as an important part of your master plan.

Positive Mental Attitude and Success

Keeping a positive mental attitude is one of the most important things you can do to guarantee success. It is a proven fact positive thinking and success are very closely related. You don't have to take my word for it, there are multiple independent studies available that can verify this fact. A positive mind is always solution conscious so it's fairly easy to see how this can be very beneficial in a business environment. I'm not going to sugarcoat the fact you will be encountering issues and problems on a daily basis: that's just business. A negative mind will dwell on these problems and that's about as far as it will get. On the other hand, a positive mind will identify and analyze a problem and then, will start to think in terms of solution number one, solution number two, solution number three, and so on until all solutions have been determined. At this point the problem has been replaced by solutions. In other words, you will no longer have a problem but you have a really great selection of solutions. Now all you have to do is select the best solution and you are free to get back to more productive tasks. I think you will agree, this positive thinking stuff is pretty special and this is only a small part of the story.

Here is a question for you: do you enjoy being healthy and stress free? I'll go ahead and answer this question for you: the answer is YES!! Positive thinking and a positive mental attitude are two of the best contributors to good health and stress relief that you will ever find. Once again, not my opinion. It's all backed by independent studies and research.

The reason: negative thinking actually triggers the release of toxins in your body which affects your immune system. Whenever you have a negative thought and you feel a bit ill, there is a good reason: it's real, your body is under attack. The really great news is just one positive thought and you are all better again. It's almost like magic except it's all backed by scientific studies.

In addition to keeping you well, I mentioned positive thinking would allow you to be stress free. That's not exactly an accurate statement because you will experience a certain degree of stress. But, you won't be able to identify it as stress. You see, this is going to be the "good stress". You know, the kind of stress which will be your source of motivation. Instead of allowing your workload to push you through the day you will, instead, be pushing the workload through the day. Because of positive thinking you will always be expecting the best outcome so there will be no issue of doubt to slow you down. Now that you no longer have obstacles in your way, you will be able to charge through the day and easily accomplish more than you ever thought possible. Remember, it's not me talking, it's scientific fact.

I have made a few comments as to how, "What and how you think can influence the outcome of a particular situation". To be sure, I experience all of the benefits of positive thinking on a daily basis. More than anything else I have noticed what and how I think in any given situation does affect the end result. In just about every case, if I expected the best outcome that's what happened. On the other hand, if I had a weak moment and did not exactly expect the best result, then that's basically what I got: a mediocre result. Now you may be thinking: "Yes, but you could expect the best outcome and something bad could happen!". Well, in this case, I am sure I at least learned a valuable lesson. You know, when something bad happens it's just creating the opportunity for something better to take its place, so what's the problem?". Bingo! Now you see how this positive thinking stuff works. Good outcome or bad, if you can determine the silver lining in any given situation it's always a great outcome.

Of course, you have to train your mind for positive thinking. However, allow me to make a very important comment before I discuss the subject of training your mind for positive thinking. To be sure, there are people out there who are natural born positive thinkers. I am elated they have this very valuable trait but they are truly in the minority. As a matter of fact, the vast majority of positive thinkers are "learned" positive thinkers. In other words, they had to acquire positive thinking the hard way. For extremely negative individuals learning positive thinking is going to be a very difficult path but, rest absolutely certain, you can do it. The most difficult obstacle is you must believe in your heart and in your mind that positive thinking is as beneficial as I (and researchers) know it is. You will also have to internalize the fact your health, wellbeing and future success will reach levels you never thought possible. If all of this sounds like it will work for you then there is no time like the present to get started. Your new life is waiting so please don't let it get away from you.

Now that you are convinced positive thinking is the right course to take, here are a few tips which may get you headed in the right direction. Keep in mind, there are plenty of books and training aids dedicated to positive thinking so I'm only going to give you a brief overview. Most positive thinking principles are fairly basic but implementation can be a bear so, be forewarned, you may have some work on your hands. I can give you first-hand knowledge of this experience since I personally had to endure this process. I am *positive* it made me a better and more productive person.

Replacement Theory

The first and possibly the most productive principle for positive thinking is what is call the "replacement theory". Simply stated it's the concept of replacing negative thoughts with positive thoughts. Sounds easy enough but it's not. Negative thoughts are very powerful and emotionally charged for some so this is when your dedication to positive thinking will truly be put to the test. At first this task will seem to be impossible but once you get that first positive thought to overpower that negative thought you have accomplished the first step toward conquering "The Beast". Once you know you can do it the next negative thought encounter will go somewhat more easily. Now the secret to this concept is to make it a habit and the next thing you know it will be like flipping a switch. The beauty of this principle is: soon the negative thoughts will simply give up and there will be nothing but positive thoughts remaining.

Self-Talk

The second and equally important positive thinking principle is using positive self-talk. Self-talk is the little voice in your head that seems to rattle on forever with all kinds of different thoughts, ideas, random discussions, and whatever else that may pop into your mind. Sometimes you can never tell what self-talk may come up with. Here is the deal with self-talk: if it's positive that's perfect and if it's negative it's got to go and quick. Allow me to differentiate between regular negative thinking and negative self-talk. Negative thinking is when an actual situation arises, say at work, and your first response is "What a disaster, I'll never be able to figure this out!". This is a real issue that is happening in real time. To be sure, positive thinking and positive self-talk are related but with a slightly different twist.

On the other hand, self-talk is somewhat imaginary and a bit elusive. These thoughts are zipping through your mind like a video game in your head. To be sure, self-talk is perfectly normal but it's the content that can be a bit of a problem. A positive thinker will perform a particular task to completion and their first self-talk moment will be; "Yeah, that looks nice, I did a really a great job!". A negative thinker will perform the same task, get the same result, and their self-talk will be; "Well, I messed it up again, I can't do anything right". For sure, a positive thinker can easily foul something up but their self-talk will be; "I guess I didn't give this my best effort, but I'm going to fix it and then I'm going to do a better job the next time!". The same situation for a negative thinker and the self-talk will be; "Okay, I give up, I quit, I just can't do this any-more!". Once again, same task, same result, it's simply a case of one person had a positive mindset and the other had a negative mindset. It's as simple as that!

As I mentioned earlier, self-talk is somewhat elusive and thoughts can zip into your mind with little to no warning. They can be hard to intercept and that's what makes negative self-talk hard to deal with. Keep in mind, I am not a professional in this field but I can tell you what worked for me. If you feel as though you are encoun-tering more negative self-talk than you prefer: be your own Best Friend! The next time you do something, make sure you compliment yourself on what a really great job you did. If you mess up just assure yourself you will fix it and do a better job the next time. This is not going to be an occasional event. You will be doing this many times in any given day until this becomes a (great) habit. Before long you are going to realize what a really special and talented person you are but, above all, make sure you remember to keep the compliments coming!

Positive Thinking People

I'm sure everyone is familiar with the term: "You are what you eat". Well I have a slight twist on that little expression. I like to say: "You become the people you associate with". I don't believe this comes as any surprise to anyone, it's just that every now and then we forget. You won't always be able to associate with all positive thinkers but it is important you identify the negative people and limit your exposure to them. You must develop "negative thinker radar". Generally it doesn't take long to identify these individuals. Their words are your first clue but it is important to take notice of their facial expressions, how they dress and even how they walk. They just seem to be worn out all the time. They are! Negative thinking has driven them into the ground. This condition is contagious so stay away whenever possible.

The good news is that positive thinking is even more contagious. To be sure, this is a "good" conta-gious. Just as you can easily identify a negative thinker, you can always recognize the positive thinkers. They are the easiest of all to identify. They stand straight and tall, they always have good things to say, they always have that confident smile, and they are always happy to see you. I think you will agree, these are the kind of people you really want to associate with on a daily basis.

If you happen to be a negative thinker or a negative thinker who is trying to become a positive thinker, please make sure you have good things to say whenever you are around positive thinking people. If you don't it might be the last time that person will be associating with you. You really don't want this to happen because every positive thinker you come in contact with, will, without their knowledge, be one of your men-tors. You will be forced into saying nice and positive things because you don't want to run the risk of losing these individuals as friends or associates. You see, when you are having positive conversations with positive individuals you are going to start feeling so great inside you will have no choice but to smile and then the next thing you know you will be laughing. Soon you will realize positive thinking is the most addictive, feel good (non) drug you will ever experience.

Reverse Filtering

This is my own term taken from a technical term "filtering" which applies to individuals who think negatively. The way filtering works is a negative thinker can receive several positive comments and then one piece of constructive criticism and they will only hear the constructive criticism. The good positive thoughts were "filtered" out and all they hear is the constructive criticism which they misconstrue as a negative comment.

Now comes my concept of "Reverse Filtering". I'm sure you have already figured out reverse filtering is the opposite of filtering. In other words, it's so positive thinkers can filter out comments from negative individuals. It's as simple as flipping the filter around and then saying good bye to negative input. I can vouch for the fact it works because I've been using it for years with wonderful success.

The reason I'm letting you in on this little secret is because you will be doing a lot of reverse filtering. In the automotive business, as with other businesses, you will be encountering your share of negative comments from some of your customers. Many, or even most, of these comments will have nothing to do with you. What you must understand is, these people are most likely upset because of the cost of the repair to their vehicle and, as a result, are taking their frustrations out on you. If you gave them a fair estimate, did the appropriate repair and did them correctly, you have done all you can do. The point I am trying to make is: you need to reverse filter all of these negative comments. Once the customer gets it out of their system they will start to compliment you. At this time you will be more than happy to allow the positive input through your filter. Please make it a point to use this reverse filter every chance you get. Not to worry, you will never wear it out.

Solution Conscious vs. Problem Conscious

First and foremost, always treat problems as learning experiences. I'm sure you know, working on automobiles is not exactly a cakewalk and dealing with customers can also be a challenge at times. All problems, whether shop related or customer related, must be resolved as quickly and effectively as possible so your utmost attention will be required at all times. This will work best if you always treat problems as opportunities. This should get you very excited because this will be your opportunity to shine.

The very first thing you are going to do is put a nice, big confident smile on your face. When you do this, you are already well over half way to solving the problem! You see, if you let the problem drag you down your mind will not be free to gather the appropriate data which will allow you to arrive at a speedy resolution of the situation.

I am confident all of the solutions to your business related issues are in this guide but, if not, you will still have sufficient information to analyze and resolve any situation that gets tossed your way. With this approach you will be shocked and amazed at how quickly and easily solutions will be coming to you. The added benefit is, you now have firsthand experience for this particular situation and when the same problem comes up again you will know exactly what to do. On the same note, if similar but different problems arise then you can use elements of one problem to solve another problem. Soon, you will have a very nice mental database of solutions to various problems. Before long, what were problems are now routine moments that you can power through without giving a thought. That's one very rewarding feeling.

The second technique for problem solving is to (1) identify the problem, (2) state the problem and then (3) completely stop talking about the problem. From this point on the focus is on the solution or solutions. If you keep talking about the problem you will be wasting your time. You already know the problem now you want answers. Now it's time to brainstorm and come up with viable answers to the problem right then and there.

Another method that works well for me is to walk away and do something else. The more I try to force solutions the more difficult it is for me to come up with answers. Which method you use depends on how you operate best.

It is most important that you *Do Not Ignore* the problem: it will not go away. When I mentioned walking away from the problem and then coming back to it, I definitely did not mean for you to walk away forever. Depending on the problem, the time frame should be a couple of hours but not more than a day. Of course, some problems take longer than others and that's completely understandable. I'm just saying don't procrastinate. Waiting won't make it any easier. Every problem will pull on you like a lead weight so the more problems the more weights. Soon, you will be exhausted. It is imperative you face off, resolve and move on.

You can be the best technician and/or the best business person on the planet and problems will happen. It's just the way it is and that's the way it's always been. Always keep in mind, its business, so don't take it personally. If you did everything right and by the book you have nothing to worry about. If you made a mistake, or did something wrong, the sooner you take responsibility for it the sooner you can get back on track and move forward. A good customer will understand and respect the fact no one is perfect and even they can stumble and fall from time to time. The sooner you "come clean" the sooner you will gain their respect back. I can assure you, when a situation like this occurs, the bond between you and your customer will only get stronger.

As I mentioned at the beginning of this section, this is only a partial introduction to positive thinking and personal development. Although this guide is dedicated to auto repair shop management, I felt this subject was essential to the success of any auto repair facility. If you already consider yourself to be a positive thinker simply treat this as a refresher course. Remember, it is very important to take any situation or occurrence and find something good in it. If you are not a positive thinking person you must start training your mind now. Any negative thoughts will only slow you down from achieving your goals. Never, ever, ever underestimate the power of positive thinking.

SECTION 2

The Building

Building Location

The first and most important rule when selecting your location is to check the zoning first! I cannot stress enough how important this step is! If the location is not zoned for automotive repair you will not be able to get a business license to operate at that address. No business license, no business: it's as simple as that. Never assume that because a building is being, or has been, used for auto repair the zoning allows for that use. The zoning could have changed or the tenant may have been operating without a license. There could be any number of other reasons for this to happen but the bottom line is you must go to the Zoning Department in the building's jurisdiction and get verification in writing! This is a very important step which can prevent devastating problems at a later date. If someone complains, you could be forced out of business because of improper use of the property. You could fight it in court but if you're operating in violation of zoning laws you will lose. Applying for a variance or zoning change could take months, or even years, wasting valuable time and money that you could be using more effectively in your business. I could preach to you for days on this subject but that wouldn't improve your automotive business so remember to get zoning approval in writing before signing a lease.

There are a few little tricks to zeroing in on the perfect location for your shop. The most important concept you want to fully understand is ***you don't need the best location.*** By "the best location" I mean buildings or properties that front on major roads or intersections. These locations are very expensive and could be a major drag on your cash flow. That said, if you are one of those extremely ambitious people who enjoys a fast paced lifestyle then one of these front line locations could be perfect for you. It will require long hours and a lot of physical and mental energy. You would first want to make sure you have a large enough building and be able to acquire enough techs to staff the shop because you will need a healthy cash flow to be profitable. The good news is, if you watch your other expenses and manage the business efficiently, you may be able to lower your breakeven point and end up with a very substantial income.

Another very important location concept which I strongly recommend is to *position yourself in close proximity to your competition.* If there are two auto repair facilities on the same street then you want to locate between them. If the other two shops seem to be doing well then you are in the right place. You see, they have already created a flow of customers that will be driving right past your door and it didn't cost you a penny. So, find the highest concentration of repair shops in your area and simply "plop" yourself right square in the middle of them. This may seem like a scary idea but I absolutely promise this concept will work like a charm.

You may ask: "How can I be so certain this will work?". Well, you are going to be better than your competition and the reason is you will have the advantage of this guide. If you follow my guidelines they won't have a "Snowball's chance in Hell" of competing with you. Sooner or later your competition is going to make mistakes and you are going to be right there to intercept their customers. Their customers are going to drive up to your shop (remember you're located next to your competition) because they figure, since you are just getting started, you will appreciate their business. And, you will!

Little did they know when they walked through your front door they would be a lifetime customer: but you did! All that's required is they walk through the front door and then you can take it from there. Really great signage will get them in the door and your neat, well-organized office, in conjunction with your expertise and professionalism, will finalize the acquisition of this new customer. The really great news is this will work the same with every disgruntled customer who comes from your competition. Just keep up the good work and you will have all of their customers. That's not nice but that's business. Your competitors had their chance so don't feel sorry for them!!

Here is another consideration when choosing a location. If you decide to locate in a rural setting where there is little or no competition you will really have to do some serious homework. This can be a very risky proposition! If there is no one doing auto repair in an area then maybe there is no market for this service. At this point, you must do a very thorough market study to determine if there is an undiscovered market. This situation actually occurs much more often than you may think.

One of the best ways to gather information is to go where the local residents socialize and start up a conversation with them. Start with social conversation and then kind of ease into the question; "So, where do you get your car repaired around here?". Their answers will truly give you a wealth of information, so listen closely. They could respond with: "Well, several people have tried a repair shop but there wasn't enough business so they closed down". Or: "There was a guy here who had a shop but he decided to retire and nobody took it over. He was covered up with work all of the time". Another response could be: "They are building a new factory down the road and people are moving here in droves so somebody better get in here and open a repair shop soon. Otherwise, these people will have to drive thirty-five to forty miles to get their car worked on". Now this is data you can use! Don't take the word of one person: you must talk to many people for verification. If you start hearing the same positive information over and over then you may have discovered an "untapped" market. So, if what you are hearing is positive, it's time to swing into action!

At this point, all you have to do is locate a suitable building in the general area. In the "Building" section I discuss the features you should be looking for in an automotive repair facility so make a note of these details. Unfortunately, a building suitable for auto repair in that particular area may or may not be available. The bad news is you will most likely have to build a new building; the good news is you will be able to build exactly what you want. Make sure to pay close attention to my recommendations for design and features because this new building will cost you a lot. You definitely do not want to make mistakes that will cost you even more. Remember, we are striving for super efficiency so don't make too many changes which may prove to be counterproductive.

Generally, constructing a new building is not the wisest decision for a startup business but sometimes you gotta do what you gotta do if your decision is to move forward. This will require a lot more money at startup and will eat up a large majority of your working capital. Insufficient cash reserves is the primary cause of failure for a startup business so don't make any fatal mistakes here. Be very conscientious! You will really need to do your homework if you decide to build so you won't be stopped before you get started. The good news is: you will now own commercial real estate and that is generally a good investment. In my particular case I first rented, and then three days shy of a year of being in business, I was moving into my new building. It was one of the very best investments I ever made.

Another very important point to consider about your location is: customers will need easy and safe entry and exit to and from your shop. If it's difficult to enter and exit the property it may not be the best location for your business. Quite often these properties have attractive rents but if customers can't get on and off the property easily and safely, it's of no value to you or your business. It may be a high traffic location but customers will drive past your repair shop in favor of another business with better accessibility.

It's important to note, many locations are easily accessible during midday hours but will be impossible to navigate during morning and evening rush hours. This is a problem since customers typically drop cars off in the morning when headed to work and pick up in the evening when returning home. Before renting a location like this you want to try driving on and off the property at random times to see how difficult it really is. If you honestly think your customers won't mind then "Go For It!". Keep in mind, when you sign a lease it's generally for five years. That's a long time to pay rent on a marginally productive location. Trust your gut because, if you think this might be a problem it probably will be, so go ahead and pay a little more rent and get the location you feel more comfortable with.

The Building Design

If you read my story in the introduction you may recall my experience working at a shop with a poorly designed building. Prior to opening my own repair shop I worked at an independent garage which was in a building that had some major design flaws. To look at the building you would never know anything was wrong. It looked exactly like thousands of other repair shops: a big box with a couple of large overhead doors. This design can easily function as an auto repair shop but it is extremely inefficient. It is all but impossible to create any kind of decent flow in a building like this. Rather than waste your time telling you what was wrong with this design I will describe the proper building configuration which will allow you to quickly and efficiently get cars in the shop, make the repairs and get them out.

Oddly enough, the perfect building can be a big box like the one I just described, but that's where any similarities with a poorly designed building end. The most important feature of the perfect building is that, instead of a couple of overhead doors, *the perfect building will have many overhead doors so every tech will have a work bay with a fully functioning overhead door.* This feature is critically important because each and every tech must be able to enter and exit the building on a second's notice and without interference. This feature is essential for maximum efficiency. The only bay that doesn't require an overhead door is the unit repair room or equipment room but it would be quite beneficial if it did.

These overhead doors should be a heavy gauge steel preferably without standard windows. Standard windows can create several security issues. For instance, they make it easy for someone to look in and view your tools and equipment for possible theft. Once they've taken a look they can return later, break the window to help gain access to your building and then steal your tools and equipment.

I will be the first to admit, windows do make it very easy to take quick peeks outside to refresh your memory as to the status of vehicles. Windows help prevent the need for opening a door especially in the winter when open doors can lead to excessive heat loss. My best suggestion is to use the smallest windows you can find that are just large enough to look out but too small for someone to get their hand or arm through. In addition, it must be tempered glass or Lexan with a reflective one way film applied. This way you can look out but no one can look in.

Another option is to simply install metal or solid colored plastic hinged flaps (inside) on the windows for the overhead doors. This way you can lift the flap to look outside when needed without the necessity of opening the door. But, when the flap is down no one can see inside. If you are renting the building, this could be the best way to resolve this issue. Whatever your final solution, make certain passersby, especially the afterhours ones, will not be able to view the contents of your shop. Eliminating temptation will go a long way towards helping to eliminate a theft problem.

Another consideration is multiple doors are a source of a great deal of heat loss in cold weather. In colder climates these doors should be well insulated and airtight. If you are trying to save money and can't afford insulated doors then make sure the doors can at least be equipped with very high quality air tight seals. Studies have shown, given the choice, air tightness will prevent heat loss more effectively than insulation. The good news is you can purchase un-insulated doors and then install insulation at a later date. In reality, you will most likely be renting a building so, in this case, I would strongly recommend installing air seals and insulation in all of the existing overhead doors. The best method for insulating overhead doors is to install Reflective "R" insulation and then, rigid Styrofoam™ insulation over it on each panel of your overhead doors. I have used a combination of these two materials on the overhead doors in my shop and experienced results superior to factory insulated units so it's definitely worth the effort.

Most everyone is familiar with rigid STYROFOAM™ insulation but may not have heard of Reflective "R" insulation. Reflective "R" insulation is an aluminized bubble wrap looking material that comes on a roll. It can be purchased at building supply stores, roof centers and anywhere insulation is sold. It is also an extremely easy material to work with which helps speed up installation. One detail you may want to be aware of is that, due to the slight additional weight on the doors, the lift springs may require some adjustment.

It may seem kind of odd to you that I am discussing the subject of insulating overhead doors when I should be talking about auto repair shop management. I think most will agree, anything that reduces expenses and increases your net profit would be a great management recommendation. Keep in mind, insulating your overhead doors is a onetime moderate expense while heating a repair shop is a potentially large monthly expense. Heating expenses for auto repair facilities in areas with colder climates can be a serious budget buster. This one recommendation could easily save you twenty to forty percent on a monthly heating bill. This can make a huge difference in your bottom line making it a detail which cannot be ignored. You must always be conscious of expenses and creative ways of reducing them to a minimum.

After all is said and done, you may be thinking: "These multiple overhead doors are a pain.", and you would be somewhat correct. Initially they are a fair amount of work but the benefits will more than offset the inconvenience. The primary problem with fewer overhead doors will be the inability to get vehicles in and out of the building quickly and efficiently. Keep in mind, anything that slows your techs down is going to be reflected in lost revenue as the result of reduced efficiency so you can see that's not going to work. Remember, you are in business to make money!

One of the greatest benefits to having an overhead door for each tech is you can generate more revenue with less square footage. With the multiple overhead door configuration, every square foot which is under the building roof will be available exclusively for the repair of vehicles. The reason is there will be no need to maneuver vehicles inside the building in order to access the lifts. You will be doing this from outside the building.

Now let's talk about the "one door in, one door out" configuration. This is also called the "center aisle" or "side aisle" configuration. The center aisle configuration has an aisle or passageway down the middle with work bays and lifts to the left and the right as you drive through the building. The side aisle configuration is similar to the center aisle configuration except that, instead of having work bays on both sides of the passageway, they will only be on one side or the other.

There are a few problems with both the side and center aisle configurations. With the center aisle configuration you lose use of one third of your useable square footage, and with the side aisle configuration you will lose approximately half of your usable square footage. The reason is the aisle or passageway area cannot be used for auto repair because once a vehicle is disabled in the aisle area you are shut down. No entry and no exit means nobody is going anywhere and vehicles will not be completed and delivered to customers.

Now you can see why the multiple overhead door configuration is a much better arrangement. Quick entry and quick exit is critical for maximum efficiency in an auto repair facility. Don't forget the added benefit of greater production with less square footage. This is truly a winning combination.

Time for a reality check: as I have mentioned several times before, you will most likely be renting a building to start and then, soon after, will be expanding into your own new building. Unfortunately, the likelihood of you finding the perfect building to rent will be slim to none. Under no circumstances are you to be the least bit discouraged with this situation.

The important feature to remember is: *your location has priority over building configuration* so, if you wish to agonize over anything let it be your location. Keep in mind, the building must have a reasonable flow pattern if it is to function as an auto repair facility. If you can't determine a decent flow pattern then you should simply pass on that particular location. Acquiring the right building and location will be one of your more difficult business decisions so you will have to exert some serious mental effort to get this very important phase of your auto repair business right. Rest assured, if you do your homework, you will find the right building in the right location and soon after, your business will be up and running. Before you know it, you will be reviewing plans for your new perfect auto repair facility.

Just so you know, I will be discussing more specific details concerning the building in "The Shop" section so make sure you read that before making any final decisions on the building.

Parking

All parking arrangements are different but the most important thing to remember is *parking must be very orderly*. You *Must* put a lot of thought into the most efficient layout which will allow customers to enter and exit the property quickly and easily and not experience any unnecessary hazards. Another important feature to remember is: *never put customers in a situation where they will have to back up.* Backing up is when most mishaps occur. This may seem like a very insignificant detail except for the fact, if a customer has a little "fender bender" on your property, they will remember your shop as the place with the "difficult parking" which caused them to damage their car so they won't be coming back. If that's not bad enough, they will be reporting this to their friends. This would not be a big deal except their friends could be potential customers who you will never see. You wouldn't think something as simple as parking a car would be such a big deal but, rest assured, it is. Parking issues can cause more problems than you could ever imagine so a great parking plan is essential.

One way to use parking to your advantage is to position customers' cars based on their repair status. As soon as a customer arrives and a repair order is written the car should be quickly moved to a designated area for *cars to be repaired*. This would normally be an area behind the building but, whatever the location, make sure the vehicles are easily accessible and in a safe and secure area. If you position all of the cars to be worked on in a designated location your techs won't have to waste their valuable time searching everywhere for a car that is in need of repair. In this case, the vehicle can be retrieved quickly and efficiently without any confusion and will get in the shop quickly so repairs can begin as soon as possible. This may seem like an insignificant detail but a few minutes lost here and there will add up quickly. We all know time is money so anything that will save time will generate more revenue for you. Once the car has been repaired and thoroughly road tested it should now be parked in the designated *ready for pickup* area. It is important to note, the *cars to be repaired* area should be totally separate from your *cars to be picked up* area.

The reason I recommend this simple step is *it helps dramatically in assessing work progress.* You see, if a vehicle is parked in the *ready for pickup* area and a customer calls about the status of their car, within a matter of seconds you can tell them "It's finished!". You don't have to check paperwork or ask any questions, just take a simple glance and you are done. By the same token, if a car is in the, *to be worked on,* area or in the shop, once again, a simple glance is all it takes to determine the status of the vehicle. This is invaluable to the person responsible for managing workload because he or she can quickly look at the parking areas and assess progress.

At this point, you may be thinking to yourself: "Is this organized parking notion really that important?", and the answer is, "It most definitely is!". To put this whole concept in a nutshell: you will have enough important issues to deal with on a daily basis, so organized parking will get rid of one of them. Having this organized parking setup will allow the manager to make adjustments to the schedule or to notify customers of progress on their vehicle very quickly and easily. The manager can then make periodic calls to customers updating them on the progress with their vehicle which is a very definite confidence builder for your customers. It will also dramatically reduce those awkward moments at the end of the day when you have an office full of customers and you have to explain to one of them their car isn't ready. Your other customers will hear this conversation and wonder if they will be the next one this will happen to. Parking cars in an orderly, organized fashion will allow the manager to access the situation in a timely manner and then notify the owner to prevent this awkward situation. Always remember, it's always the little details that make the big difference and this is definitely one of those "little details".

The Office

Normally you wouldn't get this opportunity but, this is your second chance to make a great first impression, so consider this your lucky day. If you recall, your first opportunity for a great first impression occurred when your customer drove up to your neat clean building with its organized parking area. Then, the accessibility to your office, appearance of the reception area and how the office is managed reinforced this first impression. The following are important recommendations which will assist you in achieving this goal.

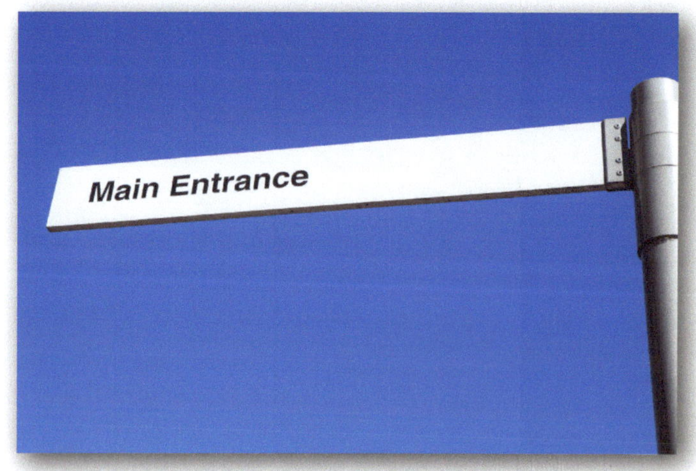

Effective Signs

Let's start with your signs. Your customer just parked their car and is ready to come into the office and reception area. Even if it's their first visit they will be able to walk up to the building, open the door and walk into the office with the confidence they are in the right place. The reason they will be able to do this is because you placed nice, legible, easy-to-understand signs in the appropriate locations. Great signage is one of the best investments you can make so don't scrimp on this one. As I mentioned, "clear" and "legible" are the keys to effective signage. Fancy signs with lots of graphics can look really nice but have little to no informational value. It's very easy to make signs that are nice looking and easy to read. All you have to do is use a nice color scheme with plenty of contrast and that should be all you will need to attract attention. Keep in mind, there will not be a lot of space on most signs so pick your words carefully. Too many words can confuse matters so selecting a few key words is the very best way to convey your message. Remember, simple is better!

If you don't have effective signage, new customers may stumble and fumble trying to locate your office and may feel awkward because they can't figure out where to go or what to do. Right away you have created an uncomfortable moment for your new customer which will affect their confidence in you and possibly in themselves. If this happens, your second chance at a great first impression just went in the toilet.

Once your signs are in place, it's time to test their effectiveness. Have a trusted friend, or friends, come to the shop. With signs in place, have them drive up to your business as though they are a customer and pay close attention to their comments and suggestions. Let them know up front their honesty is more important than your feelings so they shouldn't hold back with constructive criticism. Remember, you are in business now so this information could make a tremendous difference in how your shop performs on and after opening day so ask them point blank; "Did you feel comfortable and confident when you drove up to the building and walked into the office?". They will be very honest with you because they want to see you do well, so listen to their comments and then, implement their suggestions.

In addition, once your business opens it will be important for you to listen to customer comments and then make more adjustments. They may say something like: "Your signs sure made it easy to find your building and your reception area". They may say: "I couldn't find your building because the sign was turned the wrong way.", or, "I couldn't find your reception area because the sign wasn't clear". You will hear any number of comments from your customers so make sure you write them down. If you hear the same or similar comments from customers multiple times then it's time to take action. Believe it or not, your customers are very interested in your success because they trust you and they want to know you will be there when they need you.

Office Area Layout

Now, your customer made it into your reception area and they seem to be happy, so you are sure you have made a good second "First Impression". So far, so good!

Now that they have made it into the reception area, be sure they are looking at nicely painted walls, good lighting, clean, attractive floors, well-organized desks, and a neatly dressed staff. Under these circumstances, there is no way this customer would ever consider going anywhere else. The message: spend some bucks on your office. It will be a wise investment!! You see, your customer will rarely go into the shop area so when they see a neat and orderly office they will assume the shop area will be the same. And, it *Will Be*!

The most desirable office arrangement is to have a reception area, a separate waiting room area and a private office. Most of your business will be transacted in the reception area but you will be using the private office quite a bit also. The reception area should be used for general service writing and vehicle drop off while the office will be used for those occasions when privacy is important: especially for customer comfort. The waiting room will be for those occasional customers who elect to remain at the shop and wait for their vehicle to be repaired.

It is important the office, reception and waiting area should look crisp and clean. It should have a homey, yet professional appearance. It is also very important all furniture and fixtures are properly coordinated and in new or like new condition. If new or like new furniture and fixtures will place a burden your budget there is another option.

For the guys, I'm going to make this very easy for you. It's time to call on your lady business associate or that special lady in your life. All you have to do is determine the budget and within about two days she will have the office, waiting and reception areas looking like a million bucks. The ladies seem to have a special knack for finding super deals on furniture and then assembling the total package with amazing results. As for the guys, your primary function in this scenario is to lift and carry and do what she asks you to do so you can quickly and efficiently get the office area up and running. Remember, your objective is to keep your startup costs as low as possible while, at the same time, having a neat, orderly and professional office, reception and waiting area.

The Reception and Service Writing Area

This is the area where you will be greeting customers, consulting with customers and, then, writing repair orders. The reception area should always be inviting with nice lighting and appointments.

Counters are a surprisingly complicated issue. I had counters in the reception area at my shop but that may not have been the best choice. Counters tend to create a barrier between you and your customer and, as you know, this is not a desirable situation. I mention later the fact barriers are an undesirable feature in your private office so the same concept applies to your reception area. You see, we are back to that all important concept of customer comfort. This is what I should have done in my shop:

For the actual reception area I would recommend a moderately sized desk with a comfortable office chair. This desk should have a nice appearance but does not necessarily have to be fancy. To be sure, this reception desk would be best located between your waiting room and your consultation and service writing rooms. In addition, it should be in close proximity to the front door. Keep in mind, this will be the first thing your customers will see when they enter your building so this is exactly the time when your second chance for that great first impression begins. This reception desk should be a fully functioning work area but it must be neat and orderly at all times. It must also be staffed by a knowledgeable individual. There is a really good chance the receptionist will be multi-tasking and could possibly be away from the desk. In this case a nice door chime will alert the receptionist so they can quickly return to greet the customer. If the receptionist does happen to be seated at the desk they should stand up and walk around the desk to greet the customer. I can assure you the customer will be impressed!

Depending on the size of your repair facility and the availability of office floor space, I would recommend constructing one or more cubicles large enough to accommodate a medium sized table with three or four chairs. These will be your consultation and service writing areas. Once again, use a medium sized wood table or a small conference room table and three or four chairs in each room. Depending on the configuration of your consultation rooms, round tables may well be the best choice. This would allow for multiple individuals to sit at the table and share an equal vantage point. Unlike your private office, these cubicles should have a very open look with lots of glass and a conventional interior door. At this point you and your customer will be discussing needed repairs and, with the exception of basic service charges, there should be little to no discussion as to costs of repair so privacy will not be an issue. The important thing to note about this open look is you don't want customers to feel as though you are trying to hide anything. By using this open cubicle concept you will show your customers you have respect for their privacy and, at the same time, you will be showing them you are also making a gallant effort to be transparent.

I have been using the term "cubicle" to describe your consultation/service writing rooms but the word "cubicle" generally refers to a square room. Please feel free to use any configuration you prefer for these rooms. Depending on the space you have available, these rooms could all be different shapes. I would say, determine the most efficient and cost effective layout for your consultation/service writing rooms and they should work fine.

Another very cost effective consideration for your service writing areas is to purchase pre-made, free standing panels. In reality, you will most likely be renting your building to begin with so using these panels can potentially save you quite a bit on construction costs. In addition, you can take them with you when it's time to move to a new or larger building. Although these panels are very cost effective, I would not classify them as cheap. The really great news: these panels are readily available used at most of the larger office furniture supply stores. The condition can vary but they will generally have a good selection of panels in excellent condition and at a fraction of the cost of new. I consider these panels an excellent solution to your consultation/service writing rooms so I would call this a preferred option: at least in the beginning.

I would highly recommend flowers, pictures and other special appointments in your consultation/service writing rooms which will add to that nice, inviting, homey look. To be sure, I can't stress the importance of customer comfort enough! When you treat your customers like friends, you will be astounded as to how much more positively they will respond to your recommendations. Now, with this said, it will also be much easier for you to handle many other customer related situations.

The Waiting Room Area

The waiting room should closely resemble the living room in your house. It should have a sofa, several chairs, coffee and end tables and whatever other appointments you think would look nice. Also, make sure you include a nice TV in the waiting room. I would suggest tuning it to your most popular local channel. In addition, I would highly recommend installing a Wi-Fi system for the waiting room. Most, if not all of your customers use computers for work so Wi-Fi will allow them to accomplish work related items and entertain themselves while waiting. They will be much more relaxed because they won't feel like they are wasting time while waiting for their car to be repaired. The other bonus for you is your customer most likely won't be bugging you every fifteen minutes wondering when their car will be ready. And, don't forget the free coffee and snacks! That said, remember to do whatever you think is necessary to make your customers feel comfortable and welcome during their brief stay at your place of business.

I think everyone reading this guide is fully aware of the importance of an efficient and well-equipped repair shop area. Your reception and waiting room areas are equally important. These areas will be your command center so they must function like a well-oiled machine. The efficiency and effectiveness of your shop will be a direct function of the efficiency and effectiveness of your reception area. Remember, if you run a tight ship up front you will have a tight ship in the shop area and this is one of our primary goals.

The Private Office

As the owner and manager, this will be your command center. This is where most of your business and financial decisions will be made. This will also be your private "think tank" and problem solving area. But, the most important use of your private office is dealing with customer related issues.

To begin, a nice private office is essential for good customer relations. Quite often you will encounter issues with cars when the repairs are more serious than originally thought. It's no surprise some auto repairs can get quite expensive. This can be a tremendous burden for many customers. This is when a private office or consultation area is so important. If discussions are held in a private office a customer's personal financial issues won't be broadcast to everyone in the waiting room or reception area. The customer will be more relaxed knowing they will not have an audience and, as a result, can more easily make the decision to proceed with the repair on their vehicle. Keep in mind, customer comfort is extremely important so a private office is essential for good customer relations.

Occasionally you will have a customer complaint and you will want to address this in a private setting so it will not distract your other customers. Even the best managed and operated businesses can have a dissatisfied customer from time to time but you don't want the whole world to know about it. Having a private office will allow you and your customer to be very open and honest with your discussions. On a rare occasion you may have an irate customer who could be very loud and could make comments about you or your auto repair facility which would be quite untrue. You do not want your other customers to hear these comments because they may misconstrue them as being true and this could create some doubt in their minds. In this case, an issue with one customer has now created potential issues with other customers. I'm sure you will agree, since your goal is to increase your customer base, this scenario is never acceptable.

A private office is also very helpful for conducting your normal everyday business. There are all kinds of business related issues which require a certain degree of privacy. One of the first things that comes to mind is discussions with your bookkeeper. As you may guess, these conversations should be strictly confidential. This is privileged information between you and your bookkeeper that no one, other than your accountant, is to know about. Your private office is definitely the place for these communications.

Other important business related uses for your private office could be discussions with employees and associates, parts suppliers and insurance claims adjusters, etc. I think you get the message: there will be many, many important discussions which will require a private environment and, if not, the whole world will know all the details of your business.

It is important that your private office is soundproof. This requires an additional expense but is well worth it. If the conversations can be heard through thin, poorly insulated walls then your "private office" is not really a private office. There are a number of ways to soundproof a room and a good licensed contractor can give you some options. Based on my experience, here are a few comments and suggestions that may be helpful.

One of the simplest ways to soundproof your private office is to use a standard insulated exterior entry door and have the walls be a thicker six inch (known as 2"x 6") wood stud configuration with insulation. This insulation should be the sound deadening type. This is very basic construction and is also the least expensive and most cost effective route to take. This configuration should work fine provided your office is not located directly next to your reception and waiting area.

If your private office does happen to share common walls with your reception/waiting room areas then soundproofing of the walls may require a bit more effort. There are several soundproofing systems on the market but my preference is to use materials that are readily available from a local building supply store. The most economical method of achieving this super sound proofing is to use a double 2"x 4" wood stud wall. Generally, wall construction is a single 2"x 4" configuration so this double 2" x 4" stud wall will increase wall thickness for added sound proofing. These walls will be independent of each other so you can have whatever amount of separation your contractor feels is necessary. Do at least an eight inch wall thickness with a twelve inch wall thickness being the maximum. Once again, follow your contractor's recommendations and proceed accordingly. Keep in mind, this wall cavity should be filled with good, high quality sound deadening insulation. If you follow this recommendation, you will be able to have a party in your office and no one would ever know!

It's best to not have interior windows or a glass door in your private office. Customers in the waiting room may be able to view the body language of a customer who is in consultation and detect there is a problem. Keep in mind, body language can speak louder than words so, if one of your customers in the waiting room is able to observe a dissatisfied customer in your office, all of the sound proofing in the world will be of no benefit to you or your business. The movements and gesturing of the customer in the office will be a dead giveaway to your customer in the waiting room, there is a problem. At that point, they will start to worry they will be the next to have a problem.

Naturally your private office must be very professional and organized looking. A successful image is very important. With this in mind, have a nice desk with an office chair and then two chairs for the other side of the desk. This arrangement will be used primarily for all of your regular business discussions and will not be used if you are dealing with a customer complaint or concern. Using this arrangement would create a barrier between you and your customer and, in a high stress situation, is not a desirable arrangement.

When dealing with customer related issues, it is essential you stick with the theme of customer comfort. So, create a nice personal sitting area in your office slightly away from your desk area. Have two or three nice matching chairs similar to what you would have in a living room and then place these chairs in a circular fashion so they will be facing each other. Another arrangement would be to have a small sofa and a nice matching chair with the chair facing the sofa. Now all you need is a small area rug in the middle to tie it all together and you will be set. Whatever arrangement you choose just make sure everyone is comfortable and facing each other with no "barriers". Remember, the ladies will be able to figure this out in no time so the office arrangement task should be a breeze.

The most important thing to keep in mind: don't have too much seating. Remember, dealing with a customer's issues should be a one on one or, at most, one on two meeting which means family and friends are not included. This is extremely important because allowing additional individuals into the meeting will almost guarantee you will not come to a resolution. Keeping seating to a minimum keeps participation to a minimum. This one office arrangement detail will, by itself, do more to dramatically increase the possibility of a speedy and amicable resolution than just about anything else you can do. Of course, you must also use the proper customer relation techniques. The combination of office configuration and good customer relation techniques is the winning formula for solving customer related issues.

The Office Mascot

Meet the official greeter! I hope you are a pet lover because there is nothing like having a cute and friendly pet in the reception or waiting room area to lighten the mood and brighten the day for everyone. I love all pets, but a dog would be my best choice for a reception area mascot and greeter. Nothing will break the ice with your customers like a friendly little dog dancing around the reception area wagging its tail. Now granted, not everyone cares about pets but I am sure the vast majority do. In a year's time I seriously doubt having a pet in the reception area will be objectionable to a single person. I can absolutely assure you a pet in the reception area will certainly lift the spirits and improve the mood of almost all your customers and your staff!

For most, this information comes as no surprise. You will be amazed at how much better your work day will go when your pet comes to work with you. You should also allow your employee/associates to bring their well-behaved pets to work. Remember, the operative words are "well-behaved". Too many pets who aren't will make the place look like a zoo and that could be counterproductive. We definitely don't want that to happen!

The most important aspect of the "pet in the office" concept is concern for their health and wellbeing. All pets should be well trained and well managed. They should always respond to voice command. Pets should always stay in the office area unless accompanied by a responsible person. Never allow pets in the shop area. Even though you will keep the shop spotlessly clean, the possibility of a mishap with chemicals still exists. Antifreeze is a very deadly killer and drinking a small amount will cause a very slow and painful death for your mascot. As a responsible auto repair shop owner, you will not allow this or any other incident to occur on your watch. So remember, bring your well-behaved pets to work with you but keep them in the office for safety.

SECTION 3

The Shop

Service Bay Size

The size of your service bays is extremely important for the efficient repair of automobiles. I have experimented with several different service bay sizes and configurations and the optimal size work area for a single car or light truck should be 12 feet by 24 feet. It is important for this 12 foot by 24 foot workspace to be totally open and unrestricted. Ideally these spaces should be continuous and connected (as in an open space) but they don't have to be. Even if this space is enclosed by walls there will be plenty of room to open car doors, walk around the car and place equipment in various locations around the vehicle. The size of this shop work space is important because it will allow the tech to work quickly and efficiently while avoiding potential damage to the vehicle. This space will also allow for laying out and organizing parts as they are removed from the vehicle.

A 12 foot by 24 foot service bay may seem quite large but will fill up very quickly when you begin repairing or servicing a vehicle. Keep in mind, vehicles will be all different sizes but a space this size will accommodate something as large as a crew cab pickup truck. These crew cab vehicles can be more than 20 feet in length so the available space in the service bay will be maxed out. This would be the largest vehicle that could be serviced in this 12 foot by 24 foot space. I won't go into truck bay sizes at this time since our focus in this guide is on auto repair.

Ceiling Height

Ceiling height is very important. Too low and you run the risk of damaging a customer's car when raising it on a lift; too high and the building will cost you an arm and a leg to heat. Ceiling height will be determined by what you decide to use the service bay for. If the bay is going to be used for a flat service bay with no lift then of course the ceiling height can be lower than a ceiling for a bay with a lift. At this point, you will have to figure out how many lifts you are going to have and where they will be located to achieve maximum efficiency.

In all honesty, if you have to rent a building, and you most likely will when you start, you may not have much control over ceiling height. But, if you are looking at a building to rent and it looks like the Super Dome when you walk in the door then you may want to walk away. In colder climates it could cost a small fortune to heat.

In an automotive shop, I suggest you look for a slightly lower ceiling height as opposed to higher: just not Too Low! *The most important thing to remember is, you will need to contact the lift manufacturer and verify the minimum requirement for ceiling height.* When raising a vehicle on a lift, techs must be sufficiently aware of the vehicle as to not cause any damage but, as we all know, sometimes accidents can still happen. Another option would be to install a limit switch on the lift so it won't go too high.

The main reason ceiling height is such a big issue is summed up in the question; "Do you want to spend three hundred dollars per month for heat or do you want to spend fifteen hundred dollars per month for heat?". You may think I am exaggerating but I assure you, I am not! If you plan on operating your business in an area with a moderate to cold climate, fifteen hundred dollars a month for your heating bill may be on the low side. Of course, marginal insulation and air leaks can account for a lot of your heating bill but high ceilings can gobble up more of your heating dollar than just about anything else. This situation can potentially put you out of business before you get a good start. If you do manage to survive this expense at startup it will continue to be a huge drag on your bottom line for years to come. As an option, you could use a strategy of opening your business in the early spring which would give you about six months to build reserves to help pay your heating bill for the upcoming winter.

As you can see, you definitely must have your thinking cap on when you are trying to determine floor space usage and the associated ceiling height. There is a fine line between too much ceiling height and not enough. Too low and the building will not function for auto repair; too high and your heating expense is going to take a huge bite out of your bottom line. Of course, unless you build your own building there most likely will not be a perfect situation when it comes to ceiling height. You will; however, need to make an informed choice when renting or eventually designing your own shop. Make sure you pull out the tape measure and put on your thinking cap! Ceiling height is an important detail which can either add to, or subtract from, your bottom line. Remember, you are in business now so saving money through reduced expenses is just as effective as earning money.

Flooring Considerations

A clean, attractive, painted floor in your shop can improve the efficiency of your lighting and give customers an overall impression of a well-organized, well-run automotive business. But, once you hear all of the specifics you may want to pass on this process. I can't say I would blame you. That said, I highly recommend bright, clean, painted floors in the shop area!

The most important bit of information I want you to fully understand is this: *do not use regular concrete floor paint.* These products are not designed to hold up to everyday automotive traffic or the associated oil, gasoline and solvents that come with them. The best choice for an auto repair shop floor is *epoxy paint.* There are a number of very high quality epoxy floor paints on the market so do a little research and select one which you think will work best for you. Make certain you select a well-known brand name. These epoxy paints are quite expensive so brace yourself for sticker shock!!

Painting the floor in an automotive repair facility can be a large task. It is far more complex than the painting of walls. Paying a professional to epoxy paint your floor will be quite expensive so you may want to do this process yourself. Painting a shop floor is most definitely not rocket science but it is hard work. Make sure you have sufficient reliable help because you are going to need it. Depending on the floor space, two or three hard working people should be able to get the job done very efficiently. The process will most likely take two to three long days with a day or two between each procedure to allow for drying and curing time. The most important thing to keep in mind is: the shop should be completely empty in order to get this done quickly. It is possible to do half of the shop, wait for the appropriate cure time, and then do the other half. If you plan carefully, this method can work fairly well but is far less efficient than doing the entire floor at once. The procedure varies slightly from one paint manufacturer to the other but they all follow the same basic process.

The first and most important step is to prep the floor surface. This means clean, clean, clean! Different manufacturers have their own cleaning solutions but all are very harsh and require safety precautions. The process will require scraping, sanding and scrubbing by hand. Failure to follow cleaning instructions carefully will have a serious negative impact on the performance of the floor finish. Unfortunately, you only have one opportunity to get this right because you haven't seen work until you have to strip this epoxy floor paint off and do it over again. The paint materials are expensive and you really don't want to pay twice for them. So remember, get the surface clean, clean, clean before applying paint.

Once you've completed the cleaning process, there are a few important steps which you must take. First and foremost, you must allow sufficient time for the moisture introduced during the cleaning process to fully dry. This could take a day or possibly two depending on conditions. If it's winter you should have heat and fans going and if it's summer just make sure you have plenty of air moving. Summer drying time will be affected by humidity so take this into consideration. It's very important the floor is completely dry before the painting process begins.

Once the floor is completely dry, it's time to start working on the paint. Temperature is critical for good adhesion of epoxy floor paint. The manufacturer will make a recommendation for the paint application temperature but, in most cases, sixty degrees would be considered a minimum. A temperature of seventy or higher is much more desirable. I would say, observe the manufacturer's recommendations in addition to using your best judgment.

Now, after all of the hard work you did cleaning and prepping, it's time for the big reward. The good news: applying the paint will be an absolute cake walk compared to the prep work. Most manufacturers recommend using a long handled roller to apply the paint and that's all "stand up" work. A little edging with a brush and you are done. Multiple coats may be required so, do what the paint manufacturer recommends and you will be looking at a beautiful bright floor before you know it.

Details like a well-maintained shop floor will impress customers and keep them coming back. I think you will agree with me, this is pretty important. A steady workload of repeat customers equals a steady, reliable stream of income.

Electrical Considerations

Each and every work bay should be equipped with at least one 110 volt electrical circuit and a double outlet. Every work bay should also have good lighting with no dark areas. These features are not required to function as an auto repair facility but are necessary for maximum efficiency. In addition to a higher profit margin, the greater efficiency will also reduce your aggravation factor. If you are constantly tripping over wires and hoses and looking for a place to plug in a cord, then sooner or later, this will get on your nerves and send your productivity straight out the window.

As I said, every work bay should have at least one 110 volt 20 amp double receptacle but that's not necessarily the best way to do things. To start, I would double that number of receptacles in each bay by placing one receptacle on one side and one on the other. Keep in mind, I am talking about two receptacles per box which will allow you to plug in four pieces of equipment per receptacle box. In my shop, I located the receptacles on each side and approximately midway of the bay. This layout worked very well for me. This configuration can be adjusted to meet your specific needs and could differ on individual bays so put your thinking cap on and think efficiency.

You should also strategically place 220 volt receptacles in various locations throughout the shop work area. This suggestion is a function of how much and what type of 220 volt equipment you may have or plan to acquire. The problem with 220 volt receptacles is they are a different configuration for different amperage requirements so it may require some serious thought as to the location and amperage rating of these receptacles. One solution is to make up some extra heavy duty extension cords. This way, if you have a car disassembled and you need to make, let's say, welding repairs and the welder cord won't reach, you could pull out the extension cord rather than move the car. If your requirement for 220 volt is minimal then the occasional use of an extension cord could be the very best solution. Keep in mind, this cord will be a trip hazard so as soon as the repair is completed, roll the cord up and store it appropriately for the next use.

Compressed Air and Air Lines

Access to clean, dry compressed air is essential for quick, efficient repairs. Lately there has been a move toward cordless electric tools but it's hard to beat a high quality air tool. Air tools, for the most part, are tougher and will keep going as long as you have air. I can't over-stress the importance of clean, dry air for the performance and longevity of air tools. Air tool performance will directly affect productivity so make sure you implement the following recommendations. Keep in mind, the primary goal in this segment is to achieve maximum performance from your air delivery system.

To begin, be certain you purchase an industrial air compressor that is capable of producing 160-175 PSI of air. Most air tools operate on about 90 to 110 PSI but have the capability of taking more pressure on an occasional basis. The additional air capability of the compressor will also be necessary to compensate for the loss in volume and pressure as the result of the distance the air must travel through the lines. In addition, multiple users will place a greater demand on the system.

Never locate an air compressor inside your building. They make way too much noise! It will be very unprofessional if you have to yell at your techs whenever you need to communicate with them. It will also irritate the techs which will, in turn, affect their concentration. This will be reflected in efficiency and productivity and this is never beneficial when operating a business. Your air compressor should be located just outside the building and hopefully not too close to one of your overhead doors.

It is important to note you do not want to stick your air compressor in a small interior room to reduce the noise. The compressor will overheat resulting in premature failure. A high quality air compressor is entirely too expensive to allow this to happen. The good news: simply placing the compressor outside will reduce noise to an acceptable level so it will not be a problem. All you have to do now is build a small shed roof cover and some well ventilated sides and you will have a happy air compressor and the noise will be greatly reduced.

I actually wanted to hear a little sound when my air compressor ran because, if it made a slightly different sound, I knew to check it before a major problem occurred. If you live in a colder climate, make sure you have a receptacle installed next to the compressor so you can use a magnetic engine block heater on the compressor crankcase area to keep the oil nice and warm. Now your compressor is really, really happy and will give you many years of trouble free service.

Now, let's talk about air lines. Your air lines should never be made of any type of metal and this includes copper. If you use black iron or galvanized pipe you will most certainly have problems with rust and condensation. If you use copper piping rust will not be a problem but you will still have ongoing problems with condensation. Metal piping is also difficult to work with and can be fairly expensive. There are numerous methods of reducing condensation in air lines but some of the more effective methods are rather expensive. So, my advice: *save yourself the additional time and expense by avoiding metal piping for your air lines.*

The two very best materials which I strongly recommend are Zurn Qest PEX™ or CPVC rigid plastic plumbing pipe. Just so you know, Zurn Qest PEX™ is the original manufacturer of this PEX product but other companies offer a similar piping material. All you have to do is go to any plumbing or building supply store and ask for "PEX" and they will know exactly what you are talking about. These materials are readily available, cost effective and easy to work with. By using Zurn Qest PEX™ or CPVC, you can do your own air line installation and save some big bucks. The additional benefit: these materials won't rust or suffer from condensation issues which, as previously discussed, is a common problem with metal piping. And, *Yes*, it will most definitely accommodate the air pressure that will be provided by your air compressor!

Zurn Quest PEX™

Installing PEX is as easy as cutting to length, slipping in some fittings and crimping copper bands. There is actually a new type of fitting on the market that uses a "slip connect" system. It takes about five seconds to make a connection and with no tools required. Once you get started you won't believe how easy this process can be. Your air distribution system could be up and running in a matter of hours. For sure, these slip connect fittings are more expensive but the ease and efficiency of installation will easily offset any additional cost. These slip connect fittings also have the added benefit of a quick release feature which means repairs to your air delivery system will be quick and easy.

CPVC Rigid Plastic Pipe

Installing CPVC is as simple as cutting to length, installing fittings and then priming and gluing. CPVC is a little more difficult to work with than PEX but is still worthy of consideration. On the other hand, since it is a more rigid material it is much easier to work with if you want nice straight runs. In other words, the finished product will have a better appearance so, if the air lines are going to be exposed, CPVC could be the better choice. They also make special fittings for high pressure applications which I highly recommend.

Here are a few details worthy of consideration: air lines should have some "fall" so whatever condensation that does form in the lines will drain to a central location. At this location you should install a collection chamber with a "ball valve" drain. It is also very important you drain the air compressor at least once per day to reduce the volume of condensation in your air lines. I also highly recommend a good quality in-line air filter/water separator.

A few more very important details: when installing your flexible "bay" air lines, make certain they all drop from the ceiling and are strategically located at each work bay. This feature is very important since it helps keep air lines off the floor. Air lines on the floor are a serious trip hazard, not to mention, each time you need one you have to bend over and pick it up. If you keep your ceiling "hose drops" a little over six feet from the floor they will be accessible but out of the way. They will also remain clean. Here is a helpful hint: in my shop we used flexible plastic "coil" lines that gave us the ability of extending to length as needed and then retract to their normal length when not in use. These coil hoses are readily available from your tool route guy or any supply house that sells air and air tool products.

Make certain all of the PEX and CPVC airlines are at least three quarter inch (¾") in diameter. This is a standard dimension for both of these materials so this size will be readily available whenever you need it. You can go up to an inch in diameter with your airlines but, unless you have an extremely long run, I don't think you will notice a benefit. The one inch materials are also readily available but are slightly more difficult to work with. Stick to the three quarter diameter material for airline piping unless a technicality dictates otherwise.

Lighting Considerations

Strategically positioned lighting can easily make the difference between an efficient, productive work station and one that is not. *If you can't see it, you can't fix it*!! One thing that makes lighting difficult is different individuals require different amounts of lighting. I personally require less light and extremely bright lights will interfere with my vision. I have worked with techs who required such bright lighting that, when I entered their work spaces, I had to squint my eyes and it would take a few minutes for them to adjust. There are other issues you will be encountering but, not to worry, there are solutions.

Your focus is on lighting which will give you the maximum amount light or lumens for lowest energy cost. Notice I said *lowest energy cost*, not *lowest actual cost* of light fixtures. We are going back to the old concept of initial cost versus cost to operate. You can purchase cheap lighting but it will cost you more to operate. In other words, you can save a little money now but it will cost you much more in the long run. The purchase of lighting is a one-time expense while the cost to operate is an ongoing monthly expense. Believe me, you would be amazed at how much a monthly electric bill can be so anything you can do to lower it is beneficial.

There are a number of good possibilities for lighting so I will start with the most efficient and go to the least efficient. I will not discuss incandescent lighting since this type of lighting is extremely inefficient and expensive to operate. It's important to note incandescent lighting will not be available in the not too distant future. This technology has run its course and newer, much more energy efficient lighting has emerged.

LED Lighting

LED stands for Light Emitting Diode. This is the latest technology in lighting and by far the most efficient. The catch is LEDs are so new the technology hasn't progressed to the point of lowering the price so they are still expensive. I'm not in any way trying to talk you out of LED lighting, but rather, get some firm pricing and do a good cost/benefit analysis and then make your decision. I can tell you as a fact, the cost to operate LEDs is miniscule. A sixty watt LED can cost as little as ninety five cents per year to operate. Granted, you will require far more than sixty watts of lighting but it's easy to see the potential for an electric bill for an entire year costing less than a couple months for other types of lighting.

Another hidden benefit of LEDs is the life expectancy. An LED bulb can easily last ten to fifteen years if not more. They can be almost maintenance free and this will mean huge savings for you in the long run. The only problem with taking the LED route will be the increased costs at startup when you can least afford it. The big question is how much of your valuable startup capital are you willing to use for a future benefit. This is strictly a judgment call on your part, but be very careful with this one, because startup capital is a very precious commodity which cannot be wasted. You will be the best judge of what you can afford for lighting so this will have to be another one of your important business decisions.

You may want to consider using a less expensive form of lighting to start with and then convert to LED fixtures when you can. It is important to let your electrician know your intentions so the electrical plan can be designed to accommodate the upgrade at a later date. One advantage to holding off on LED lighting is time and technology should substantially reduce the cost which will be a noticeable benefit to you. As I mentioned earlier, I would highly recommend doing a good cost/benefit analysis and let the numbers answer this question for you.

Discussions in the previous paragraphs do not apply to the many portable handheld LED flashlights that are presently on the market. It is important to note, these are of the personal type and should be the responsibility of your techs to purchase. The cost of these flashlights can vary greatly. You can spend as little as five dollars or as much as two hundred fifty dollars. Like most everything else, you get what you pay for so I recommend buying a more expensive unit. The guys with the tool trucks generally have a nice selection of these LED flashlights with lifetime warranties so this is what I would recommend. These lights also have rechargeable batteries which save the expense of replacing single use batteries.

Even though the techs should be responsible for purchasing their own handheld lights, it would be perfectly acceptable for the shop to purchase them and allow techs to use them as necessary. The benefit to you, the shop owner, is the increased efficiency of the tech being able to actually see what they are working on so the repair will go more quickly. Always make sure you have a good system in place for keeping track of these lights because losing one of them can get expensive. The most effective method of accomplishing this is to have any tech who is using one of these lights sign an agreement stating they have use of the light and will be responsible for loss, theft, or damage. It's not a foolproof solution but should help.

In addition to the flashlight style LED lights, you can also get the longer tube type LED lights that are either handheld or can be secured to the underside of a hood. These lights can be corded, cordless or a combination of the two and emit a tremendous amount of light. Since it attaches to the hood of a car, it can easily light up the entire engine compartment for really great visibility. These lights are very useful whenever enhanced visibility is needed so I would strongly recommend investing in several of these units.

High Pressure Sodium Lighting

High pressure Sodium Lighting has been around for a while now and has proved to be very efficient and maintenance free. They were originally designed for exterior applications as dusk to dawn lighting but were quickly adapted to other interior uses. The main concern is they give off an amber colored light that some people don't care for, but others like. My best recommendation is to locate a licensed electrician who has installed this type of lighting and visit several locations to see if you like them or not.

High Pressure Sodium light fixtures are not what I would call cheap but, at the same time, I would classify them as very cost effective. The cost is roughly half that of LEDs but the energy use is at least four times greater. Not to worry, LEDs use such a minuscule amount of electricity that four times the energy use is still quite low. The High Pressure Sodium bulbs and transformers have a very long service life so, depending on the quality of the fixtures, maintenance costs should be minimal for years to come. Assembly and installation of these light fixtures is fairly straightforward and does not require any special wiring or unusual circuits. These fixtures do not come in portable versions.

Fluorescent Lighting

Fluorescent Lighting is by far the most popular form of lighting for an automotive repair shop. It has been around for a number of years and has evolved over time in an effort to improve efficiency. It has the unique feature of being very reasonably priced and fairly inexpensive to operate.

The fixtures are not difficult to install and do not require any special wiring or tools. There is a moderate amount of maintenance but materials and labor are not that expensive. Solid state ballasts with built in starters have resolved most of the issues fluorescent lighting has had over the years. In addition, the units that are presently on the market, with their redesigned bulbs, are much more efficient, reliable and trouble free.

The older style ballasts were prone to overheating and premature failure. Another problem with these old ballasts was they wouldn't function properly in temperatures below fifty five degrees. Repair shops can drop below this temperature from time to time so, if you decide to go with fluorescents, make sure you specify solid state ballasts. I believe most of the old type ballasts are off of the market by now but I recommend playing it safe by confirming they are solid state. In addition to being more reliable, solid state ballasts are more energy efficient. This, in addition to more efficient and brighter bulbs, makes fluorescents even more desirable than ever before.

Compact Fluorescent Lighting

Compact fluorescent lighting, otherwise known as CFL, has become the standard, lowest cost replacement for the old obsolete incandescent bulb. These are the bulbs with the spiral configuration that can be screwed into a regular light socket. They have been on the market for a few years now and are taking the lighting market by storm. If you have applications that require a standard screw-in light bulb the CFL is the best way to go. Long life and reduced energy consumption make the CFL a good cost effective method of resolving many of your lighting issues.

Fluorescents are a very good choice for a shop in the startup phase because they can lower initial costs and maintain ongoing costs at an acceptable level. If you are renting your building it will most likely already be equipped with fluorescent lighting. They may work fine in which case all you will have to do is flip a switch. Let's hope that's the case but if not, make sure the landlord agrees in writing to have all lighting in good working order prior to occupancy. This will help you save a fair sum of money which can be applied to other phases of your startup plan.

Lighting Placement

As you may recall, I discussed the work bay size and configuration as a twelve by twenty four foot rectangular area. I have found the most efficient placement for lighting is to have a fixture in the very front, one in the very back and one on each side of the work bay. If your rectangular bays are side by side then the lights on each side will service adjacent bays. If your light fixtures are sized properly this configuration will supply more than enough lighting to allow your techs to quickly and efficiently repair an automobile. Standard sizes include two tube, eight feet in length and four tube, four feet in length. You may have a special situation so evaluate your needs and adjust accordingly. Use a little common sense and logic and the right solution will come to you.

As a side note: by painting the walls and floor in very light and bright colors your lighting volume will double. As discussed before, floor painting can get a bit pricey (still highly recommended) but basic wall painting is very inexpensive for labor and materials. The job will not require any custom paint work so inexpensive latex paint and minimum wage labor is all you will need to accomplish this task. I would strongly suggest applying a darker color paint on the bottom four feet of the wall so possible discolorations will not show up as badly. Another really nice benefit to painting the walls with a sharp color scheme is the shop will look neat, clean and professional. Customers will be impressed!

Unit Repair and Tool Room

This is where all equipment and specialty tools will reside. The unit repair and tool room should be about the same size as a full size service bay: twelve feet by twenty four feet. This will be more than large enough to accommodate all of the tools and equipment necessary to serve an average sized auto shop. The best arrangement is to place all equipment around the perimeter of the room with the center being an open area. This configuration will allow techs with larger components such as transmissions and engines to navigate and work without interference.

If you are fortunate you may be able to rent a shop that already has a unit repair and tool room set up and ready to go. Even then, you will most likely have to make modifications to suit your own individual needs. If you have to build your own unit room then you can build it exactly the way you want it. For security reasons, I would strongly recommend having the room completely enclosed and locked. You are going to have a lot of money tied up in all of your equipment so it is important you keep everything secure. You should also have enough room to lock up other valuable items when you leave work at the end of the day.

I would also recommend installing an oversized entry door for accessibility. My preference would be four feet wide. A standard door opening is about three feet so a four foot door would be a special order or custom made unit. This door is well worth the additional expense so make sure your unit repair room has this feature.

The important thing to remember is to have plenty of electrical receptacles and air drops in your unit repair room. These features are just as important in the unit repair and tool room as they are in the service bays. Minimal or no air and electrical in the unit room means you are always looking for a place to connect electrical or air tools. If you try to improvise by connecting to other areas in the shop you will continually be tripping over cords and hoses, not to mention the fact you will be wasting much of your valuable time.

The best arrangement is to place four "gang" (two receptacles per box) electrical receptacle boxes spaced no more than eight feet apart on the wall around the entire perimeter of the room and about four feet off the floor for best accessibility. Receptacles should be 110 volts with a capacity of 20 amps. Install two or three separate dedicated circuits to accommodate the electrical demand when the shop is running at maximum capacity. You will also need at least one 220 volt receptacle which could accommodate a welder. My best suggestion is to consult with your electrician for their recommendations.

As with the work bay air installation, I strongly recommend air hose drops from the ceiling. The best method is to run hard piping using three quarter inch (¾") PEX or CPVC along the ceiling. Run one main trunk line down the length of the room in the center and then add lines across allowing for at least four, or even six, air hose drops around the perimeter of the room. Make sure these air hose drops are about four feet off the wall so they're accessible but won't protrude into the work area. Generally speaking, you want the air hose drops to be very close to equipment and workbenches but not interfere with their operation. You can use a straight piece of rubber hose for an air hose drop or a flexible coil hose which allows for greater versatility.

Another configuration that works fine is to install hard lines along the wall. Once again, using three quarter inch (¾ in) PEX or CPVC would be the material of choice. This method is the standard "old school" approach and, for some, has worked for years. If this system works for you and your techs it is definitely okay to use this method. The accessibility to air is fine with this configuration but, once again, your air lines will constantly be in your way. This could directly affect your efficiency and productivity when working in the unit repair and tool room. As we all know, anything that affects efficiency and productivity also affects your bottom line. This said, if you still think wall mounting air lines will work best for you then go for it.

You can use a combination of straight air lines and flex lines depending on your individual needs. As always, use your imagination when designing your layout because your application may have different requirements.

Later in this guide I discuss the fact work benches are not permitted in the shop service bay area. Now, if you must have workbenches the unit repair and tool room is where they will be located. You will notice I called them "work benches" not "junk benches".

Remember, with this setup everyone in the shop will be sharing the unit repair room and everything in it. This includes the workbenches. If they are covered with junk and debris they will not be functional. The top surface must be kept clear at all times. Depending on what the workbench will be used for, some minimal supplies can be stored on top but only if used on a regular basis. Always make sure workbench supplies don't get out of hand and everybody will be happy; not to mention the fact, everyone will be able to get their work done.

EPA and OSHA Regulations

I guess you were wondering when this subject would come up. I hate to say it but EPA and OSHA are a reality and are here to stay. It is very important you adjust your thinking on this one and accept the fact they are actually here to help. On the outside chance you are not familiar with these two organizations, EPA stands for Environmental Protection Agency and OSHA stands for Occupational Safety and Health Administration. These are both government agencies.

One agency is charged with protecting the environment (EPA) and the other with on-the-job safety (OSHA). Auto repair facilities fall well within the guidelines of these two agencies so you must be very familiar with, and comply with, all of their applicable regulations if you expect to remain in the automotive business. I will not even attempt to quote all of their regulations: that would be another book. Your best bet is to go to the individual web sites for EPA and OSHA and get it straight from the "horse's mouth". This way you will be assured of getting accurate and up to date information. Any confusion in this area can lead to stiff fines and penalties and you really don't want to go there.

The Environmental Protection Agency

Automotive repair shops contain and produce a lot of hazardous chemicals: solvents, oil and antifreeze to name a few. This is perfectly acceptable. You could not operate an automotive facility without these materials.

Although EPA regulations are very complex, I will make a brief attempt to simplify and make them a little less "scary". If you have properly stored chemicals, solvents, oil, antifreeze, etc., on your premises and they are either, in a *sealed container provided by the manufacturer* or, in an *EPA approved sealed container*, you have absolutely nothing to worry about. *You are in compliance!!*

Now, let's take these same substances and allow them to either leak, spill or be poured on the floor, ground or, heaven forbid, down a drain. Now you have a problem. Accidental leaks or spills are a fact of life. The responsible thing to do is to follow *EPA guidelines* and do a thorough cleanup. If you dispose of the waste as directed you will be in compliance and you will still have nothing to worry about.

This next scenario is when you start getting into trouble! When a hazardous substance is poured or dumped on a floor, on the ground, or in a drain or otherwise disposed of inappropriately, you are now treading on very thin ice. Generally speaking, inappropriate disposal is either intentional or the result of ignorance of regulations. Whatever the case may be, it's totally unacceptable behavior. The big problem with this occurrence is you, the owner, most likely had no knowledge of this incident. The next problem is, whether you had knowledge of this incident or not, you are still responsible. This is where educating your shop staff really pays off. Training is the key to avoiding issues such as these. The fines and penalties could easily put you out of business.

Pouring hazardous substances down a drain, specifically a public waste water disposal system, is the most unacceptable of unacceptable behaviors. This should never, ever happen!! Even though this waste is thoroughly treated, these chemicals can still end up in streams and rivers. Treatment plants treat for normal contaminants but have no way of dealing with hazardous material removal. The automotive industry generates a massive volume of hazardous materials and, if left unchecked, will have a tremendous impact on our environment. As responsible auto repair shop owners we can never let this happen.

In addition, many of the municipalities have special sensors installed in their waste water lines which are designed to detect hazardous waste. They are strategically positioned so they can pinpoint the exact location these materials entered the system. If you think you can *lock the doors* and *turn off the lights* and get away with this, your luck may just run out on you. Do not consider pouring hazardous materials down a drain!!! Sooner or later you will get caught and the disposal fee to a licensed company will be a tiny drop in the bucket compared to the fines and penalties you will have to pay for improper disposal.

There are a number of reputable, licensed waste disposal companies out there so you can pretty much take your pick. Believe me, they will most likely be knocking on your door before you are even open. Make sure they are *EPA licensed* and then compare price and value and go with the best deal. The license is extremely important because if they are not licensed, and they are hauling waste and or hazardous materials from your business, and have an accidental spill, you are still responsible. So, for your protection make absolutely certain they are *EPA licensed.*

While we are on the subject of toxic waste materials, there is a related subject that requires very strict attention on your part: the disposal of waste oil and antifreeze. This is definitely under close scrutiny by the EPA. I will not publish any recommendations or guidelines in this guide concerning this matter but I will refer you to the EPA website for exact details. These guidelines are subject to change from time to time so you'll have to check the EPA website on a regular basis. Make absolutely certain you use *EPA approved containers* for your waste oil and antifreeze and then have it removed by an *EPA licensed* waste disposal company.

Sometimes a friend, a customer, or someone off the street will come in and want some waste oil. There are all kinds of questionable uses for waste oil. There are many people who use it as a wood preservative. Some people spray it on the ground to cut down on dust. Others use it to burn in fabricated "oil drip" stoves. I could go on with examples but I think you get the idea. People have a lot of uses for waste oil: all of which are totally unacceptable.

If waste oil or any other hazardous waste material from your shop is in the hands of any unlicensed individual, no matter what the reason, you are still responsible. If, in the process of transporting these materials, there is a spill you are responsible. Under no circumstances are you to allow any hazardous waste to leave your premises unless it's in the hands of an *EPA licensed* waste handling company. Once you have handed over your waste products to an *EPA licensed* waste handling company your liability has ended and that's the position you want to be in when it comes to hazardous waste.

I keep talking about waste oil because you will be generating more waste oil than any other hazardous waste material. Now, if there was a way to use it for your benefit then I'm sure you would agree that would be fantastic. Well, this is your lucky day because there is a useful and productive way of dealing with waste oil.

It's called a *waste oil burner*. It will dispose of your waste oil while, at the same time, heat your shop. Now, that's a concept I'm sure we can all live with. The only flaw with this idea is if you live in a warmer climate a waste oil burner won't do you much good. The waste oil burners I'm referring to are definitely not the old homemade drip units. These are truly state of the art machines set up specifically for burning waste oil. That said, please don't get any bright ideas of retrofitting a standard oil furnace because you will really have your work cut out for you. The operation is very similar but there are some distinct differences so take my word for it, don't try a conventional oil furnace conversion.

The most important feature to note is an approved waste oil furnace is extremely clean burning so you will not be polluting the atmosphere and that is a huge benefit. Keep in mind, you are legitimately disposing of waste oil and heating your shop at the same time. This waste oil won't cost you a penny but it will definitely save you big bucks on your heating bill. Don't forget, you made all that money on those oil changes and transmission services so, where I come from that's a really good deal.

Okay, I hope this information helps with making sense of all of the complex EPA regulations. They are quite involved but a little common sense will get you a long way towards understanding what these regulations are trying to accomplish. Preserving our planet for future generations is very important to me and I sincerely hope it's important to you. At the end of the day I hope it is said of the automotive repair industry; we did our part to preserve the environment of this great planet.

The Occupational Safety and Health Administration

Now, let's see what OSHA is trying to accomplish. To start, you have a team of professional automotive technicians whose responsibility it is to repair cars and get them out on the front line for delivery to the customer. After all, that's how you make money in this business. Let's say you have an unsafe situation in your shop area and one or even two of your best techs are injured and can't work. Where is that going to put you? I can assure you it won't be good and that's not the worst part. Remember, your techs were injured which means pain and suffering: not to mention the hospital bills. What a mess. All you want to do is get on with business and not have these problems.

Now you can see why there are guidelines for workplace safety. You and I would never, ever allow unsafe conditions in our repair shops: that's a given. The average person could walk in off of the street and go into an automotive repair facility and spot unsafe conditions in a matter of minutes. It's really not rocket science. I guess you can see, the excuse of: "I didn't know" will never fly!!

The next logical question is: "If unsafe conditions are so obvious then why do we need laws dedicated to workplace safety?". The answer is: human nature and economics. The human nature part is our tendency to say: "I don't have time to correct the problem now: I'll do it the first chance I get". This is otherwise known as "procrastination".

The economics aspect is it costs money and takes time to make the corrections. Unfortunately, many people in business see this as time and money that could be used to generate even more income but never seem to considering the serious consequences. Now you can see why safety issues are quite often observed but not remedied.

Now that you have this knowledge, you will not allow unsafe conditions in your shop. As I have mentioned in several locations in this guide, there should be a lady and a guy working as a team and, as owner-operators of any given auto repair facility. Once again, ladies, you have been given another task, and a very important one. Your new title to add to your other titles is, "Superintendent of Workplace Safety".

I have no idea how you ladies do it but you can spot unsafe conditions from a mile away. It has to be built into your operating system because it works perfectly every time. With all due respect, you may not fully understand why a condition is unsafe but your "women's intuition" says something is wrong and it needs to be corrected and now. The next step is to delegate the correction to your shop team leader and give a strict deadline for when this task is to be completed. Be very polite and tactful but assertive. If you recall, at the start of this section I mentioned the ramifications as the result of an injured tech *Never* has a good ending. The sooner the hazard is corrected the better.

Here is another option. If the unsafe condition is of a technical nature requiring a licensed electrician, plumber, or other type of contractor then call an appropriate licensed specialist for the task and have them make the correction as soon as possible. Let them know the health and safety of your shop staff is at stake so time is of the essence.

As a side note: you will have a certain number of customers who will be in the building trades. Get to know these people very well and, better yet, make sure you extend an extra favor to them from time to time. I can assure you there will be many times you will need their services so put your best foot forward and stay on the good side of these individuals. Many will understand and respect your concern for shop safety and will come out after hours to remedy an issue. You may even be able to trade services with them which could result in savings for both.

Well, we've come this far in the segment on OSHA and shop safety and I don't believe I've mentioned OSHA once. As with EPA regulations, there is not enough space in this guide to include OSHA regulations. You absolutely must visit the OSHA website to thoroughly review their regulations. Even though workplace safety is mostly common sense, there are details that are important to know. Read and understand, and if anything doesn't make sense, contact an OSHA official or an authority on OSHA regulations for clarification. As you may well know, ignorance of laws and regulations is no excuse so my best advice is read, understand and then implement.

Even though OSHA is responsible for enforcing workplace safety they honestly should not have been placed in this position. Workplace safety should now, and for always, be the responsibility of the business owner and especially an auto repair shop owner. I really want to see auto repair facilities and their owners be held to a higher standard with regard to workplace safety. I also want to see the auto repair sector set the standard for workplace safety by having the least number of injuries for any industry. I would love for the automotive industry to have a track record of zero injuries but that would make me a dreamer. If being a dreamer could actually put an end to workplace injuries, well: *I'm a Dreamer!*

Shop Organization

It goes without saying, if you don't have a well-organized efficient shop work area you may as well not be in the auto repair business. If you plan on making the big bucks your shop has to operate like a well-oiled machine. You must have highly trained techs working in a clean, uncluttered environment and with the latest state of the art equipment. In addition to this, you will need an innovative game plan or strategy that will keep the work load in constant motion.

From the time the vehicle enters the shop until it leaves, the focus must be on the goal of getting the car properly repaired as quickly as possible and delivered back to the customer in a timely manner. This is a very deliberate process that requires you and your team to be highly focused. To a certain degree, you will be under pressure and stress for most of the work day. This is a very positive occurrence that will cause you and your techs to perform to maximum potential.

I always enjoyed the quick energetic pace. For me, it was more like a competitive sport than work. If you keep moving at a rapid pace the momentum will keep you moving forward. Solutions will come to you much more easily because your mind will be conditioned to respond quickly when problems do occur. To make this happen you must have a well thought out system and plan of action.

First and foremost, the shop must be *clean* and *clutter free*. When I say clean and clutter free, *I don't mean kind of clean and kind of clutter free, I mean totally clean and clutter free!* This comment may sound totally absurd for an automotive repair shop but it's actually quite necessary. It's as simple as a trash can with a broom and dust pan at each work bay. Trash and debris go straight in the trash can, not on the floor and then in the trash can. It is perfectly understandable that dirt and rust from cars will end up on the floor: that's why the broom and dustpan are there. Clean it up as soon as it happens and that way you won't be walking around in a little mess turning it into a big mess. The same applies to liquid spills and possibly even more so. Oil, antifreeze, grease, and brake fluid, can make a horrible mess if left unchecked: not to mention the slip hazard. What we did in my shop was to place used, dirty (but not oil soaked) shop towels in a special fire proof bin and then used them to wipe up liquid spills. At that point they were appropriately discarded. We always kept several containers of solvent on hand to do the final clean up. Of course antifreeze is water soluble so a little water and a quick wipe up resolved that issue.

Oil absorber was a banned substance in my shop. My theory was: I already had a mess so why would I want to make a larger mess? Apply oil absorber to one small oil spot and the next thing you know it's all over the shop. The worst part is, it would end up in the customers' cars. If you wipe up the liquid spill with shop towels to begin with you will be done in only a few minutes. In addition, if you use oil absorber it could be several hours before it absorbs the liquid and then you still have to clean up the mess: not to mention the remaining stain on the floor.

Even with your best efforts the floors will, over time, collect dust, dirt and oil residue. The solution is simple: soap and water! In my shop, once a week, and normally just before closing time on Friday, we got out the hose and floor cleaner and went to work. Everyone pitched in. This was a quick thirty minute cleanup. We would move the equipment enough to keep it from getting wet; wet the floor, applied concrete cleaner, scrub, and rinse. The process was quick and easy and the shop looked fresh and clean for the upcoming week. Cleanup was actually a very happy time for everyone. It was always close to closing time, the weekend was near and everyone was working together as a team. And, the pace was somewhat slower with little to no pressure from the stress of deadlines from working on cars. Clean up was always a very relaxing end to an otherwise hectic week.

Once a month, about an hour before closing time on Friday, we deep cleaned the shop. This time we rolled all of the equipment out of the shop and thoroughly scrubbed and cleaned every nook and cranny. In cases of bad weather we moved all equipment to one side of the shop, thoroughly cleaned, then moved everything to the other side of the shop and repeated the process. It was impressive! The big reward was, once a month the shop looked like the day we moved in. An additional benefit was the boost in morale as the result of a clean shop. Techs were proud to be associated with the operation and they would make it a point to tell all of their friends about how neat, clean and well-organized the shop was. As a result, most of their friends became loyal customers. This is how you build your automotive repair business into a thriving enterprise.

Another little detail that saves time and effort is installing heavy duty wheels on everything in the shop. All equipment, to include difficult to move items, must be on wheels. One of the reasons is related to the cleanup process. In order to do an efficient cleanup you must be able to quickly and effortlessly move all obstacles. Those thirty minute Friday cleanups could have easily taken an hour and a half if shop equipment had to be moved without wheels. Even if we had a minor spill the ability to move a single piece of equipment would greatly speed the cleanup process allowing us to get back to work more quickly.

Another benefit of wheels on equipment is the ability to move the equipment to a vehicle as opposed to moving the vehicle to the equipment. In many cases the vehicle may be disabled which would make it quite difficult and time consuming to move. Keep in mind, time is money and our ultimate goal is to keep moving forward as quickly and efficiently as possible.

An additional advantage to mobile equipment is there will be times when you simply want to rearrange the shop. You may have a great idea that will improve shop efficiency but, without wheels on your equipment, will take some time out of your busy day to perform the task of rearranging this equipment. This could cause the rearrangement process to be postponed which will cause a delay in improved efficiency. This little bit of added efficiency may be exactly what you needed that day to get all of your customers' cars completed and delivered. Remember, delivered cars means money in your pocket!

Another way to keep the shop neat is to place nothing on the floor except the wheels of your rolling equipment. Parts, whether old or new, should rarely, if ever be placed on the floor. New parts should always be placed with the vehicle either on the passenger side front floor or under the hood depending on where the parts will be installed. This is a sorting process that will prevent the confusion of parts getting mixed up or lost resulting in a progress slow down. Also, the tech never has to search for parts. When they are assigned a vehicle all they will have to do is go to that vehicle, confirm the parts are correct and begin installation. This said, there will be cases where, due to size and weight, parts will have to be placed on the floor.

Immediately upon removal, all old parts should be placed in a special bin. This bin should be located in the shop close to the reception area so the customer can view them on demand when the vehicle is completed and picked up. Hold on to the parts for at least a week in case something comes up later. There are laws in many states which allow for fines upwards of ten thousand dollars if you are unable to produce the old parts which were removed from a customer's vehicle. Needless to say, you would be very wise to check your state laws regarding this issue and take special care with replaced parts. If you used remanufactured parts then hold on to the old part, or core until after the owner has inspected it and the vehicle has been delivered. After your state's required holding time for old parts has been satisfied, you can send them back to the remanufacturer.

I'm going to catch a lot of flak over this next concept, but I can assure you, I will be 110% correct and accurate when I say, "No workbenches are permitted in the individual work bays!!". By work bay, I am referring to that nice 12 foot x 24 foot work space discussed earlier which is dedicated to the repair of automobiles. The only work bench, or benches, for the entire shop will be located in your unit repair area or room. The only two items that will be allowed in the service bay will be a small to medium sized tool box and a heavy duty rolling cart. No exceptions.

I was first exposed to this concept of no workbenches in the work bay area while working at a European new car dealership. I'll never forget the first day I went to work at the dealership. I had my tool box set up and ready to go and I didn't have a work bench in my work bay. When I asked the shop manager about workbenches he informed me they were not permitted in the service bay area. When I asked why not, the shop foreman announced in a strong German accent; "Our floor space is much too valuable to be occupied by a three foot by five foot junk collector!". That response caught me off guard but, as I thought about it, he was exactly right. Apparently there are studies that verify a service bay without a workbench can generate more revenue than one with a workbench. It seems as though the workbenches got in the way and slowed the techs down. Within a few days of no work bench I was quite relieved that monstrosity was no longer in my way. I could actually tell I was more productive. You can bet I added that detail to my list of really great ideas to implement when I was ready to open my shop.

Have no fear, there are solutions to the no workbench dilemma. Remember, there will be workbenches in your unit repair room so if you really need a workbench you will have one. The first and best solution to this problem is something we will be discussing in detail later. It's our large heavy duty rolling shop cart. I would recommend a cart of a size not greater than two feet by three feet. It is very important you invest in carts that are of the highest quality. I must admit, even with the best carts we made a few modifications to make them more durable. The most important modification was to add a piece of three quarter inch plywood with a neoprene rubber mat to the top tray area. This added the additional strength needed to accommodate the abuse which the carts sustained on a daily basis.

The primary function of these carts is to serve as a place to put your hand and power tools while working on a car. My technique was to evaluate the particular vehicle and the repair to be performed, then pull the necessary tools from my tool box and lay them out on my shop cart. The tool box stayed in a safe location on the perimeter of the work bay while the cart stayed next to me in an easily accessible location and my tools stayed off the floor. Always remember, ***if it doesn't have wheels, it doesn't touch the floor.***

Another primary function of the shop cart is to transport large or heavy parts. You may have to get a new part that was delivered, you may have to take an old part for customer inspection, or you may have to get a part to the unit repair room to rebuild or repair. Whatever the case may be, your cart must be there when you need it. It is one of the very best time and labor saving devices you will have in the shop. If you use your shop cart as you should, you will be "running the wheels off of it".

Tool boxes are another important consideration. Many techs like those nice "Aircraft Carrier" tool boxes. You might think they would make a wonderful and perfect workbench but you'd be wrong.

Earlier in this guide, I mentioned the optimal size for a work bay which was profitable, efficient and cost effective was 12 feet by 24 feet. I also mentioned this bay size would give you and your techs good, unrestricted work space around an average size vehicle and would allow the techs to make quick and efficient repairs. Now, the first question that pops into my mind is this: "If you have this nice work bay dedicated to the repair of customers' cars, and you park this monster "Aircraft Carrier" tool box in this space, where the heck are you going to put the car to work on it?".

These tool boxes are great status symbols and good tax write-offs but they sure do get in the way when you are trying to work on a vehicle and make money. I will have to admit these tool boxes are extremely secure so that's a definite benefit. My best advice is to park your big beautiful baby of a tool box in a safe but accessible place and use it for tool storage. Then, purchase a small to medium sized base cabinet and top box that will stay in the work bay with you.

One advantage of this smaller tool box is it's more maneuverable. If you are striving for super efficiency, your techs will be doing a lot of traveling around the shop with the primary goal of getting all of your customers' vehicles completed and delivered before closing time. No one is going to have a permanent work space. In many cases a customer's car will be placed in a bay where a vehicle has just been completed and delivered. In this case the tech will stay put and the car will come to him or her. But, let's say a tech is working on a car and progress is held up. You and your techs want to keep moving forward and make money. So, if you have an empty bay or a bay that has a vehicle in need of repair you can send your next available tech with their nice new portable tool box to that bay and have them get to work on that car as soon as possible. You have a lot of cars that need to be delivered by closing time and none of your customers want to hear any excuses, so make sure you assign your available technicians to whatever vehicles that need to be repaired.

This concept could be a hard sell for most technicians but once they start moving around the shop, work will be much more refreshing and exciting. Most technicians have come up through the ranks with the mentality of only working on one vehicle and in only one bay so the concept of moving around the shop and working on multiple vehicles may be difficult for many techs to wrap their heads around.

You will; however, have to keep close track of which tech performed which service on each car but that's easy enough to do. All you need to do is have the tech initial each item on the repair order upon completion of the repair. This way you will know who did the work and who will receive credit for the repair. This process does require effective communication skills but this is not a problem. In the section dedicated to developing an effective shop team, one of the primary objectives is to select team members with excellent communication skills. Problem solved!

As you can easily see, great shop organization is essential for achieving "Super Efficiency" and, "Super Efficiency" is essential for achieving maximum profits! Never lose track of the fact your primary goal for your shop is to get cars in, repair them quickly and efficiently and get them to the "Finish Line" for customer pickup. And this, my friends, is how you make money in the auto repair business!!

The Right Equipment

The right equipment strategically located in the shop area is crucial to the efficient operation of your repair facility. If you have little equipment or equipment in marginal condition then the decision to open an auto repair shop may not be your best choice. The equipment you choose will be a "make or break" decision for your business. If you chose to be a cheapskate, profits will suffer and so will you. If you opt for nice, well-maintained, "state of the art" equipment, profits will soar and so will you. Here are my recommendations:

Vehicle Lifts

A vehicle lift is one of the most effective, efficient pieces of equipment in an auto repair shop. There are very few repairs that do not require getting under a car. For all of the technicians out there who are reading this guide, you know working under a vehicle that is jacked up and on jack stands is a royal pain. In addition to being a pain there are safety issues and that's not to mention the inefficiency. I guess you can tell I'm not exactly thrilled with an automotive repair shop that is not equipped with vehicle lifts.

I can tell you firsthand what a bad decision not having lifts can be. When I opened my shop I decided to go without lifts in an effort to save startup costs. I was certain lifts were not necessary because when I was a kid growing up I worked on lots of cars without a lift so I should be able to do it now. I considered working on a car on jacks and jack stands my workout program calling it "constructive exercise" because at the end of the day I felt as though I had been lifting weights for eight hours. That was not altogether bad until one day I remembered, I was in business to make money and that business was definitely *Not* running a fitness gym. Something had to change.

The primary motivating factor for getting a lift was, I seriously needed help and it was almost impossible to find a qualified tech who would work in a shop without lifts. That was the "straw that broke the camel's back!". I kicked and screamed for a while and then I broke down and got one lift. I couldn't believe I was wasting so much money on a piece of equipment I really didn't need.

It took about two weeks or so for the lift to come in and then a couple of days to set it up. Since the primary purpose of acquiring the lift was so I could get a decent tech to help with all of the work, I didn't even bother to use it myself. Finally one day there wasn't any more room in the shop and the lift bay was all I had left so I decided I'd go ahead and use the lift to make sure it worked. As you may guess, the rest was history. As it turned out, I was able to work so quickly and efficiently with the lift I didn't even need help: at least for a while. I estimated my productivity went up at least thirty percent or more. Within three months I had more than paid for the lift through extra profits and that same lift was going to last for many years to come. That lift I thought I didn't need, turned out to be a really great decision.

There are many choices for vehicle lifts but I'm going to dramatically narrow the search so you can more easily make the right decision. You will be making many decisions so I hope this information will help take a portion of the pressure off so you can concentrate on other equally important aspects of your business.

There is one style of lift you definitely do not want to purchase. I'm referring to the "in ground" variety of lift. To be sure, they are still available new but are quite expensive. This type of lift was used almost exclusively for many, many years with great success. As a matter of fact, up until about thirty years ago, it was the only type of lift you could get. They had many nice designs but they also had some huge drawbacks.

The hydraulic cylinders that move the lift up and down were buried in the ground and had a bad habit of rusting out and leaking. The lift manufacturers were fully aware this could be an issue as the units aged so a rust proofing material was applied at the factory. Problem solved, right? Wrong! The manufacturers failed to realize that, at the time of installation, the construction work crew wasn't really that concerned if the rust proofing was accidentally scraped off. This meant the hydraulic cylinders could potentially rust through resulting in hydraulic oil leaking and contaminating the surrounding soil.

Now enters the Environmental Protection Agency. To be sure, I will not begin to even attempt to give you all of the details of what you would be required to do to remedy this situation, I'll just say it's another book and a very long one at that. I have briefly covered this subject in "The Shop" section of this guide so I will spare you any additional details at this time. I'll leave it at this: its way more time and money than you ever want to spend on anything like this. To be sure, this problem has been corrected in the newer units and is no longer an issue.

The environmental hazard is the primary issue with in-ground lifts but there is more. There is a substantial expense involved with the installation of an in ground lift. If they are installed in an existing building the concrete floor must be cut and removed. Then, the soil must be extracted before the lift can be placed in the ground. Once it's installed you will have to run air lines for the control valves and more concrete must be cut and removed. You will spend a lot of money and do a lot of work and now it's permanent.

This brings to light another problem: the building you are in is most likely rented so now, when you are ready to expand there is a good chance you will be moving to another location. Trust me, it will not be cost effective to remove your lifts and take them with you. Unfortunately, you will be placed in the position of walking away from a substantial investment and there is not a lot you can do about it! Now you can easily see what a really bad business decision in-ground lifts can be. So, solution: no in ground lifts!!!

Above Ground or Surface Mount Lifts

This will be the style of lift you will be shopping for. An above ground lift is basically a rather large steel framework with a set of swing arms on both sides which support the vehicle when raised and lowered. These lifts are, in most cases, hydraulically operated with a cable system incorporated in the mechanism. It is a fairly basic system with little variation. The more expensive lifts have a more elaborate mechanism but the end result is the same. Push the lever one way and the car goes up, push it the other way and it comes down. In reality, this is all we are looking for in a vehicle lift anyway.

Make absolutely certain you measure ceiling height accurately prior to ordering your lifts. Different brands and models come in slightly different heights so ceiling height and lift height are two very important dimensions to remember. On a related issue, make sure you don't have an interference issue with an overhead door. Overhead doors can throw a monkey wrench in the works as badly as inadequate ceiling height so look out for this and any other obstacles.

Another important consideration is the thickness of the concrete where the lift base fastens to the floor. Most lift manufacturers recommend the slab be at least six inches thick. The problem with that thickness is concrete slabs are normally four inches thick. The only time a slab will be six inches thick is when it was specified at the time it was poured that an above ground lift was going to be installed at that location in the shop. The point I really want to make is this: unless otherwise specified, a concrete slab is four inches thick. Now the dilemma is what to do.

You could do what most people do and simply install the lift and forget about it. Another option is to cut a (approximately) two foot square section of slab out where the lift mounts to the floor and pour fresh concrete. This time the concrete should be much thicker and be similar to a footing for a house. This is a fair amount of work but, you would definitely not have to worry about the lift mounting flange coming loose or the slab cracking.

The third option would be to contact a structural engineer, have them inspect the slab and get them to decide if it's safe or not. If the concrete slab appears to be in good condition they will normally sign off and give you the go ahead. This is your very best option.

To start, you may want several different styles of above ground vehicle lifts depending on what kind of service you will be performing. For general auto repair you want a lift that has a capacity of at least 7000 pounds but a 9000 pound capacity may be the most cost effective. There isn't a huge price difference and the extra capacity will give a bit of additional safety factor and that is a feature that should never be ignored. If you are fairly sure you will be working on mostly small to medium size cars then a 7000 pound unit should serve you well. Keep in mind, your business model may say you will be working on small to medium size vehicles but, in reality, you want to be able to accommodate larger vehicles from time to time. It would be a real shame if you opted to save $500 to $1000 dollars buying a smaller lift and the day you set it up a $4000 job came in and your lift wouldn't accommodate the vehicle. I don't know about you, but I think I would start to cry.

I'm not sure how many lifts your budget will allow, but buying multiple lifts of different weight capacities could be a consideration that may give you more lifts at a slightly reduced total cost. The only drawback is this would require you to plan your strategy when staging vehicles for different lifts. You want to be careful to not tie up a higher capacity lift with a smaller vehicle. This could prove to be a juggling act but having lifts of varying capacities will allow you to accommodate a much wider range of vehicles.

As a side note: these above ground lifts are somewhat intrusive so you want to make certain you have enough room to accommodate multiple lifts. A technique I like is to alternate or stagger lift positions. This will put a little distance between each lift which will give you a bit more working room. Remember, you have to navigate with tool boxes and equipment so a little extra spacing is very helpful.

You can find above ground lifts online for as little as $1200. To be honest with you, I think I would be a little nervous working under a vehicle that was on one of these lifts. All the while I would be trying to figure out how they cut corners to get to that price point. These units, even though they are rated for a certain weight capacity, actually don't have the reserve capacity to hold up under continuous use. Please don't be suckered in by online gimmicks for lifts. Make sure you know all of the hidden costs before you place the order because once the unit gets dropped at your doorstep it's yours. Good luck if you have a problem.

My very best advice is to buy local. In many cases local suppliers will price match online prices and, even if they don't, you are still ahead of the game. If any issues arise the local suppliers are right there to help. Keep in mind, you are in the process of starting a business and the last thing you need is some long distance customer service nightmare to slow you down. Buying local is always your best deal.

Most, if not all, of the tool truck guys who visit your shop will be able to supply you with very good lifts. They may cost a little more but they are quality built units that will give you many years of trouble free service. If you happen to have a problem they are right there by your side to take care of whatever is required to resolve the issue. These units generally cost upwards of $3500 so you can see there is a slight difference in the price. The big advantage of dealing with your friendly, local tool guy is they can offer you some really great financing. Even better, they may offer a lease-purchase agreement which basically allows you to use the equipment for a tax write-off twice: once when you make lease payments and again when you own it. Once you own it, your accountant can then depreciate the same unit. This should sweeten the deal substantially. Another option your tool guy can do is set you up with another brand name unit that will also give you many years of trouble free service at a reduced price and can, most likely, offer you the same financing.

Another logical place to locate a lift is a local equipment supplier or parts supplier. They can offer you similar deals as your tool guy. I would always recommend comparison shopping and then go with the best deal.

Floor Jacks

As I discussed earlier, there is a good chance not all of your service bays will have lifts so you will need something in the flat bays to raise a vehicle for various services. You will also need something to insure the vehicle will not fall and injure one of your techs.

Depending on the size of the vehicles you plan on repairing, you will need a minimum two ton and a maximum three and a half ton floor jack for each flat bay. Of course, we are talking about an automotive shop and not a truck shop. If the jacks are for a truck shop you must determine the size of the trucks you will be working on and then purchase floor jacks of the appropriate capacity.

This is when it is very important you purchase high quality brand name jacks. An inexpensive, off brand two ton jack will not perform like a brand name two ton jack. You see, the high quality brand name jack will have much more reserve capacity engineered into it than the off brand jack. You will notice the difference in several ways. First, you will notice the additional effort it will take to jack a car up. Second, there is a really good chance a two ton off brand jack will not lift two tons. A high quality two ton jack can easily lift two tons and possibly two and a half tons. Third, the failure rate for off brand jacks is extremely high. The framework is generally strong enough but the hydraulics just cannot hold up even under medium duty situations. This is a huge problem if someone is working under the car at the time something breaks or leaks down. In a perfect world, a jack stand would be in place but, in reality, it may not be. Meanwhile, a tech is seriously injured, in which case, your problems have only begun.

Jack Stands

If you are using floor jacks then jack stands are an absolute necessity. Never, ever work under a vehicle that is supported by a floor jack unless you have jack stands in place. Even if you use a high quality floor jack anything can happen. It could be an incident that is totally unrelated to the floor jack but the end result will be the same: someone is going to get seriously injured.

Even though jack stands are very important pieces of safety equipment you don't necessarily have to get the best jack stands available. Jack stands are a basic piece of equipment with very little to break or fail. Make sure they are rated for a minimum of two or three tons and look fairly sturdy. The best thing to do is check out a nice set of jack stands and compare price and quality and then decide if it may be better to go with the higher quality stands. It's always better to err on the safe side and go with higher quality stands.

Engine Diagnostic Scanner

This will be one of the most important, most valuable money making tools in your shop. I know I said at the beginning of this section all of the essential equipment I was recommending would be of equal importance. This may be the exception. Without an up to date scanner it would be difficult, if not almost impossible, to operate an auto repair facility. With all of the current technology and new technology there is no way to guess at the many possible problems modern day automobiles can develop. New vehicles come out every year so technology is constantly changing: not to mention the multiple updates made during any given model year. I think you can see the extreme importance of having a state of the art automotive diagnostic scanner.

Diagnostic scanners are available from multiple sources; many of which are totally inadequate as a primary diagnostic tool for a professional automotive repair facility. Auto parts stores quite often stock these scanners with individual car owners in mind. For the cost of around $150 they work amazingly well. They are accurate and will at least get you fairly close to figuring out many automotive related problems. It wouldn't be a bad idea to have one or even two of these little units on hand in the shop to use for quick scans in a case where your nice scanner is being used on another vehicle. One of the other techs can use the little scanner which will keep things moving forward. A word to the wise, don't rely too heavily on these little scanners. Use them only on the simple and easy diagnostic issues and leave the difficult problems for your professional scanner.

Now let's discuss the purchase of a professional diagnostic scanner. Professional units are not cheap but an inexpensive scanner that may cause you to miss diagnose a problem can cost you much more in the long run so go ahead and "spring" for a good reliable diagnostic unit. I believe a fairly nice basic scanner should set you back somewhere in the neighborhood of $6500 while a more advanced unit could go as high as $20,000. As you can see, there is quite a price range to deal with.

There are a number of really good options for purchasing diagnostic scanners. Many of the larger, more established auto parts stores will also sell the professional grade scanners. Generally speaking, the parts stores that supply these units are the same ones that cater to automotive repair shops so make sure you check to see what they have to offer.

The best source for professional scanners is your friendly, local, tool truck guy. They are always anxious to make good deals because their livelihood depends heavily on your success so they are motivated to make sure you get the best deal possible. They also carry a wide range of very high quality scanners in various price ranges that should fit your budget.

The less expensive units may require a little more "brain" work whereas the more expensive units tend to spell it out for you. With this in mind, if you are a good diagnostician then you can get by with a less expensive unit. On the other hand, if you are not comfortable with your diagnostic skills then, you may want to go with the more expensive version. They all work fine once you have learned how to use them.

A very good method of saving money on a scanner is to purchase a used one. This may sound a little risky but it isn't. The tool guys quite often have or can get their hands on used units all the time. This is because many of the more established repair shops will routinely purchase new equipment on a regular basis mainly because they want to stay up to date with technology but also because it's a great tax write off. I have actually seen repair shops buy a new scanner after as few as six months of the original purchase. If the scanner is a brand name unit that has been and, in the future, can be updated there should be no problem with the functionality of the machine. Be wary of used units that are more than a couple years old. As with other electronic devices, they become obsolete fairly quickly so make sure to estimate the service life of the scanner and adjust the price accordingly.

The important thing to remember is to buy a used unit from your tool guy or from your professional parts supplier. Buying from an individual could be risky. You may not know the condition of the unit or it could be stolen. Only purchase a used scanner from an individual when your tool guy or the parts house guy is familiar with the history of the unit and considers it to be a good deal. Oddly enough, these guys are very helpful along these lines because most likely the person selling the used unit is buying a new scanner from them. In addition, they have helped you get a scanner at a good deal realizing you will want a new scanner in the future and you will remember this good deed. It's a good sales technique that will help generate future sales for the parts and tool guys. The tool and parts guys will also look out for your best interest because they rely heavily on a long term business relationship with you and your repair facility.

Try to avoid internet sales when purchasing a scanner. Try to not be lured in by a lower price. Hidden costs and fees can easily cause the price to exceed local pricing. Even though most internet sales are legitimate, you can still have problems. Another point to keep in mind is a long distance customer service nightmare can really cramp your style when you are trying to meet a grand opening deadline. I would never consider being in the automotive business for even one day without a fully functioning scanner so make sure you purchase from someone you know and trust. Whether it's your tool guy or your professional parts house guy, always go with the person who you feel as though will be the most honest, dependable, reliable, and trustworthy. This will be a fairly sizable investment and it must function perfectly day in and day out without exception. If a little glitch does occur with your scanner you will need someone there as soon as possible to correct the problem.

Your tool guy may have the slight edge in this case since they show up on a weekly basis and can easily be contacted by phone or email with a moment's notice. To be sure, many of the more aggressive parts houses also have outside sales reps and, if this is the case, they are still a very good option. They are also easy to contact by phone or email. Stick with these two options since they have a vested interest in your success. You could say, their success depends on your success and that's always a good combination.

Professional Computer Diagnostic Programs

These programs are technically not a piece of equipment but they are a very powerful diagnostic tool. In years past this was in the form of a physical book but are now all digital. They allow you to access most of the information that is available from the manufacturer so you can easily see how beneficial they can be. The majority of information and data that is available to the technicians at the dealership is also available to any independent auto repair facility. This is true for almost all American made vehicles and almost all of the European and Asian auto makers. There are a few exceptions with several of the German auto makers. They somehow, managed to retain some proprietary information just for themselves. This is not a huge problem so not to worry.

There are a fair number of good diagnostic programs on the market so you do have some choices. As with many other computer programs, it kind of gets to be a personal preference issue. Different individuals have their own ideas as to how a computer program should function so it's whatever works best for you. The information and data should be about the same since it comes from the same source so that should make the selection process a bit easier.

The really good news: almost all of the companies who supply these programs offer a free "test drive", or trial period, so you can make an intelligent decision. Believe me, it won't take long to make a "yea or nay" decision so the process won't be that time consuming. Many of the companies who supply these diagnostic programs do not require a contract so, if you notice any discrepancies in their program, you can move on to another until you find the one that works best for you.

As a side note: you may be wondering why on earth these rather large auto manufacturers would voluntarily give up their valuable technical information to independent auto repair facilities. The answer is actually quite simple; it wasn't voluntary: it was a government mandate. Independent automotive aftermarket and aftermarket parts manufacturers, wholesalers and retailers successfully lobbied the government to require most auto manufacturers who planned to do business in the United States make their technical data available to all independent auto repair facilities. This technical information is absolutely critical to the livelihood of the independent auto repair industry.

Finally, your computer(s) will be the lifeline of your operation so if you have an older or out of date "clunker computer" you may want to consider putting it to rest. A slow, quirky computer is going to be a thorn in your side so a really great business decision would be to get a nice efficient computer(s) and things will move much more smoothly. The last thing you want is the old "herky jerky" when you are trying to run a business.

Hydraulic Press

A high quality 20-30 ton hydraulic press is another necessity in the operation of a full service repair shop. In addition to the press you will also need the associated press tools. I can't stress "high quality" enough when it comes to your press and press tools. Let me remind you, this press will have a capacity of 20 to 30 tons. Can you imagine what would happen if something broke while under that kind of pressure? A piece of broken metal could move through the air at a similar velocity as a bullet fired from a gun. And yes, that piece of metal could injure or kill a person as surely as a bullet would. So, in addition to the press and press tools I would recommend a set of protective guards. These are steel shields of different configurations that are designed for various press applications. Unfortunately few people use these protective guards so they may be a bit hard to come by. If you ever have an OSHA inspection these press shields are one of the items they will be looking for so get them and use them.

There are also hand held versions of presses designed to remove and replace components such as wheel bearings and ball joints. These are tools that look like "C" clamps, with a threaded shaft and multiple adapters. These tools work fine on many applications but, in other cases, are of little or no value. If you have situations where these work better then use them. If you have procedures that work better with your 20-30 ton floor type press then use it. This arrangement will give you a few additional options that will help keep the shop more productive and help get cars delivered on time.

A hydraulic press from an unknown or off brand source should never be a consideration. Only purchase a press with a very recognizable brand name. If you see a press with a quality brand name it was most likely manufactured to a higher standard. So remember, get a hydraulic press with a 20-30 ton capacity displaying a recognizable brand name and you will be good to go.

Brake Lathe

No professional auto repair facility should ever try to function without at least a good quality brake lathe. You will notice I'm willing to settle for a good quality brake lathe as opposed to a high quality brake lathe. In years past, brake rotors and (yes) brake drums were routinely machined with every brake job. It gave that "like new" feel to the brakes which the customer really liked. Of course, the idea is to always repair a car right the first time and eliminate those pesky comebacks.

As you may guess, over time, things have changed with regard to brake service. The primary feature that has changed is that most repair shops have adopted a policy of replacing as opposed to machining brake rotors. This is justified because many of the original equipment brake rotor manufacturers now specify "Replace: Do Not Machine". This is getting to be the standard of the industry.

In my shop I noticed machined rotors had a tendency to warp again and I noticed they warped fairly quickly after a brake service. As a result, we ended up replacing the rotors anyway. This didn't happen very often but when it did it was an inconvenience to the customer which wasn't good. The point I want to make is don't feel guilty about replacing rotors that appear to be marginal because they could be the very ones that will give you a problem. Err on the safe side and replace the rotors and move on.

There are also some rotors on the market that are absolutely not designed to be machined under any circumstances. Some of the high end cars have these types of rotors so you definitely want to check the manufacturer's recommendations prior to machining. Brake related issues can cause a person to lose their life so this is one area that requires real attention to detail.

There is another issue with some high end vehicles in that they have abrasive brake pads. These abrasive pads are designed to keep the rotors clean over the life of the brake pads but, as a result, they tend to wear the rotors out at about the same time the pads wear out. The idea is to keep the brake performance consistent over the life of the pads but the down side for the customer is the rotors must always be replaced at each pad replacement. Of course, this is not a problem for you because this is simply another opportunity for more profit. The point I want to make is: don't be surprised if a fairly late model vehicle shows up for a brake pad replacement and the rotors are also worn out. The good news is now you can give your customer a good, legitimate and logical reason as to why their brake rotors are worn out and must be replaced.

I know I should be discussing the purchase of a brake lathe in this segment but brake repair details are extremely important and deserve a little extra time. I am also trying to stress the importance of the concept of "replace" as opposed to "machining" brake rotors as it relates to the decision for the purchase of your brake lathe.

I guess the bottom line is this: due to changes in technology and the market, the thinking for now and in the future is to replace as opposed to machining rotors. Machine rotors only as permitted by the manufacturer. For this reason, I don't think it would be a wise decision to use up your valuable working capital on a piece of equipment that will see only occasional use. This said, my recommendation would be to purchase (lease/purchase) a decent brake lathe at a medium price and move on. For sure, it must functioned as designed but, it does not have to be a top of the line unit!

Battery Charger

Depending on the size of your shop, you will need at least two or more very high quality battery chargers. You are going to find a battery charger will be one of the most frequently used pieces of equipment in the shop so it must be extremely durable. For some strange reason batteries have a tendency to discharge at an alarming rate when in a repair shop. Lights and ignition switches seem to be left on fairly often especially when the shop is busy and there are many distractions. If you don't have a good reliable battery charger at your fingertips there could be a serious delay in the diagnosis and repair of a vehicle. I would say one battery charger for two techs should be sufficient. If one charger for two techs doesn't seem to be enough, you don't need another charger, you need to give the techs a memory class so they don't keep forgetting to turn lights and ignition switches off!

As a side note: be very careful as to the settings on battery chargers. Under certain conditions, setting a battery charger on "boost" can seriously damage electronic components in a car. You can easily boost charge any number of batteries without incident but all it takes is one and you will quickly learn your lesson. The problem generally occurs when a vehicle has a defective battery but you won't know until it's too late. After all, you have the battery charger connected because the vehicle won't start and a defective battery is quite often the culprit so, no "boost" settings on the battery charger.

Another battery related piece of equipment you will need on hand is a portable battery pack otherwise known as a "Jumper Box". Your portable battery pack will save the day more times than you could ever imagine. Batteries have a strange tendency of running down even in your parking lot so a nice portable method of starting a vehicle quickly is always the best way to go. A jumper box is especially handy if you have to go to the shopping mall to rescue one of your very good customers. Unless they left their lights on, they will have to come straight to your shop for a repair so you just drummed up a little more business. They will tell all of their friends about your rescue efforts so now you will be acquiring even more customers. As I always say: "It's the little details that make the big difference".

Battery Tester

It goes without saying, a nice high quality battery tester is worth its weight in gold. Batteries require routine replacement but you must first confirm it's the battery that is causing the problem. You definitely do not want to develop a reputation for needlessly replacing batteries. In many cases, when batteries run down it's the result of a faulty charging system or electrical system "draw or drain". Make sure you follow the procedure for testing batteries and if it checks out okay then go seek out the real culprit.

Welder

A welder is an extremely important piece of equipment to have on hand especially if there is someone on staff who really knows how to use it. The absolute best welding machine for an automotive shop is a wire feed: better known as a MIG welder. These are the most versatile welders available. They are used mostly for exhaust work but you can use them for any kind of welding project you like. The only limitation is the capacity of the welder itself.

For all those individuals who are not familiar with MIG welding, in addition to the welder, you will need either, a tank of inert gas or "flux" wire in order to weld. This is necessary to prevent the material being welded from vaporizing in the presence of oxygen. This gas or flux will replace the oxygen and allow for a nice clean weld. Flux core wire is available for MIG welders but I don't suggest going this route. I recommend getting the tank and be done with it. It will give a much more professional finished product.

Now you are set up and ready to weld. If you have never welded in your life, you will find this will be an extremely easy machine to learn how to use. All you have to do is locate some scrap metal and start practicing. Within a couple of frustrating hours you will be an adequately accomplished welder who can legitimately charge customers shop rate or more for welding service on their vehicle. However, unless you are a certified welder, you should never, ever weld any safety related components on any vehicle. The lawsuits could be enormous so earning a few extra dollars welding a safety related component is really, really not worth the risk!!

Determining the capacity of your MIG welder is a function of what you plan on using it for and how much you plan on using the machine. My experience has been, when you get the hang of it, you will want to weld anything and everything you get your hands on. This will allow you to repair a component on a customer's vehicle without having to replace it. Or, the component could be fine but the bracket that holds it is broken and you can simply weld the bracket and save your customer a needless expense. Its little things like this that will keep your valuable customers returning for many years to come.

Another advantage to having a nice MIG welder is, it will allow you to do some of your "Dream Projects" like building a custom street rod. Later in this guide, I suggest a project like this. The idea is, if you use the vehicle to help promote your business this project would be mostly, if not all, tax deductible. Getting your hot rod and a tax deduction at the same time is like having your cake and eating it too. So, that nice MIG welder is sounding better all the time, now isn't it?

You can start by purchasing an entry level welder to save startup expenses and then, at a later date, make an upgrade. Unless, for some strange reason, you have a very large startup budget, buying a high capacity, top of the line welder is not your best business decision. It's very important to retain all of the startup capital you can, so don't let this purchase cause you to come up short later on. I would strongly recommend against purchasing a cheap off brand or "knock off" MIG welder. Even though they are new, these units will either, not work properly from the "get go" or, will start to malfunction in about six months to a year. Keep in mind, you have cars to repair and deliver so this will not work.

As always, for your MIG welder purchase, go to your friendly tool truck guy and/or professional parts houses first because they are your strongest and closest allies in the automotive business. In addition, I strongly recommend checking out the local welding supply houses because they can also offer some really good equipment at decent deals. Most of the professional grade, brand name equipment is essentially equivalent as far as quality is concerned so go with the MIG welder that will give you the most features at the best value and you will be good to go.

The best starter welder would be one of the small 110-120 volt units. Even though they can appear to be quite small, a high quality unit can be very powerful. They should be quite heavy for their size and, in my opinion, the heavier the better. These little welders normally do not come with a cart or a regulator so that may be an additional purchase. Make sure you ask about the cart and regulator before making a decision. I decided to mount my small MIG on a standard shop cart to save a little money and, for me, it worked like a charm. I cut a hole in the top level of shop cart tray to accommodate the tank and I was ready to weld.

Once a year or so has gone by and tax time is coming up and you would like a little tax write off, it may be time to upgrade to that new larger 220-230 volt welder. Of course, your little "work horse" MIG welder will be working great (and will work great for many years to come) so it can serve as your backup unit. You never want to slow a tech down when they are trying to be productive so this is why I always recommend a backup for most of your tools and equipment.

The other advantage: you have some experience now, so you will be confident to take on a few larger welding jobs or get started on your street rod dream project. The most important benefit is you will be able to serve your customers in your facility and not send them elsewhere. It is very important you keep your customers coming to your door step as opposed to someone else's.

Parts Cleaning Tank

These tanks are generally leased from a solvent (solution) management company who also maintains and services the contents of the tank. Do not purchase a parts cleaning tank unless you have an agreement with an EPA certified company to manage the cleaning solution. By manage I mean remove used solution and replace with fresh clean solution. The EPA is very specific as to how this process is to take place and, to be sure, it is quite involved. In order to comply with these regulations it would take entirely more time and effort than you would ever want to be involved with so please let the approved disposal company handle this task. This will transfer most of the liability to the disposal company which is another important advantage. You do have a certain responsibility to the solvent disposal company to properly manage the equipment (tank) as per their guidelines. As a result, you will have a certain degree of liability but it is greatly reduced.

Bench Grinder

The good news on bench grinders is you don't have to worry about the EPA but the Occupational Safety and Health Administration (OSHA) may have a little something to say about them. It won't be that difficult to comply with OSHA because, when you purchase your nice *New* high quality bench grinder all of the safety features will be included. Make sure you install all of the components when you assemble your new bench grinder and you will be in compliance. Over time minor adjustments will be required to compensate for wear on the grinder stone. These are relatively quick and easy so they will not be a problem.

Here are a few helpful hints regarding your bench grinder. Even though it's called a "bench" grinder, I prefer to mount the grinder on a pedestal. The most desirable location would be in the unit repair room area. Locate the grinder away from your clean work areas so the debris will not get all over components that must be kept spotlessly clean. The fine dust from a grinder can wreak havoc with an automatic transmission or fuel injection component and we all know that's never good.

Another good reason to keep your grinder in its own space is for ease of cleanup. The grinder pedestal is one of the few items that will be fastened to the floor so not having obstacles around it is a huge time saving benefit when cleaning up.

One of the best places to purchase a nice heavy duty bench (pedestal) grinder is a welding supply store. They should also have the pedestal at a reasonable price so you can get both at the same time.

Vise

Yes, I'm referring to that big "clampy" tool that holds things like axles, drive shafts and other automotive components in need of repair. And, you thought I was talking about bad habits (Vice)... Well, not now: maybe later!

To start, I would strongly suggest you not purchase one of those cheap imported vises. Vises are generally used for rough service repairs and quite often are exposed to serious impact so strength and durability are very important characteristics for this piece of equipment. Even though you will be wearing a safety shield, a broken piece of metal can stray and you can still suffer an injury. An injury is never acceptable so now that cheap vise just cost you a whole lot more money than you ever thought. As a result, the best business decision is to purchase a high quality vise!!

Here are a few helpful hints regarding your vise: locate the vise in the vicinity of the "pedestal" grinder if possible. I would keep some distance between the two since there may be some longer components in the vise. They tend to complement each other so keeping them together makes good sense. A six to eight foot separation is a good recommendation. I would also recommend mounting your vise on a very sturdy pedestal. It should be much stronger than the one you will be using for the grinder. In addition to severe impact, there will be a lot of pulling, twisting and turning on parts in the vise so pedestal strength is very important.

Once again, one of the best places to buy a vise is at a welding store. They generally have a good selection so you should be able find the one that will work best for you. A medium size vise should work for most automotive repairs so that's what I would go with. So, high quality and medium size and your vise dilemma will be solved.

This pretty much covers the primary equipment you will need in the shop. There are more hand tools than I can mention in this guide but if you have the right team leader technician this aspect should be covered. Keep in mind, no single tech will have every hand tool so adding to hand tools is an ongoing process. This is why your friendly tool guy comes by every week and is always available with a quick phone call or email. Get the special tools you need and move on. They will easily pay for themselves with additional jobs so make sure you have the tools and equipment you need and get out there and make money.

SECTION 4

The Office Team

You may recall earlier in this guide, I discussed the significance of having a second chance to make that great first impression. Remember, that all important first impression occurred when your customer entered your parking area and walked up to your building and came through the front door. You may also recall this second chance to make that great first impression occurred in the office/reception area. That discussion was focused on appearance and layout of the office/reception area and, other than mentioning neatness of dress, did not include any information regarding the individuals working in that area. These will be individuals with a certain degree of automotive knowledge but, more importantly, must be very neat, knowledgeable and display exceptional "people" skills.

As you can see, your front line team must excel at all of the same characteristics you expect from your shop team. Great personality, neatness and effective communication skills should top this list. Your customers must feel confident they came to the right place to have their vehicle repaired. The best analogy I can come up with is: "Your customers should feel as though they are on vacation at a five star resort when they come to your repair facility".

A great personality is an essential trait for any individual working in your reception and service writing area. A bright, warm smile and a big: "Hi, how are you doing? My name is Alex, how may I help you today?" greeting as a customer walks in the door will do more to build your business than just about anything else you can do.

Now, I'm going to tread on a little thin ice but I will be able to get away with it. The above mentioned personality tends to describe the more outgoing individuals who you meet, better known as extroverts. These people tend to be born with this trait. I could say it's a case of, you either got it or you don't, and I would be dead wrong! Remember, I keep talking about the many judgment calls you will be faced with in the course of managing your business. Well, here's another one.

You see, the most qualified individual you could hope for could apply for a reception/service writing position but not have that outgoing personality you are looking for, so they would be immediately disqualified, right? Wrong! If this was the case it would have been necessary for me to disqualify myself when I made the decision to start working up front as a service writer at my repair facility. I most certainly did not have that outgoing personality but made the decision to do something about it.

Long story short, I simply trained myself to keep smiling, give my standard greeting and then, be polite and personable with my customers. If I could do it then anyone can do it! So, if you have that special applicant who is highly qualified in all areas except for the outgoing personality, this can easily be corrected.

It is extremely important you discuss this issue with your applicant. Explain to them in detail they are highly qualified for the position but it is imperative they must be, among other things, effective customer greeters if the business is to expand and grow. As with any new staff member, they will have a thirty day trial period but the main difference is they must prove they can perfect the greeting process and be very personable and customer care oriented.

They must also be competent in the other aspects of their position, but make it very clear customer relations will be the determining factor for them to secure the position on a permanent basis. If they really want the position, in thirty days they will master this new habit. It will now be a skill and you will find they will be extremely thrilled with their newly learned trait. They will also respect and appreciate the fact you had the foresight to see their potential and help them with their personal development. This arrangement is definitely a win-win situation which will benefit all concerned.

Okay, listen up! What I am now getting ready to discuss could be some of the most valuable information you will receive in this guide. I have alluded to this concept at several locations in this guide but now it's time to really get this point across. This message is equally for the guys and the ladies.

Your office and service advising staff should be mostly, if not all, ladies!! Now, in an effort to stay out of trouble with the ladies, I would be perfectly happy, dare I say elated, if more women were certified automotive technicians. Sad to say, my research shows very few women working as technicians in the auto repair industry. Even though I am certain women would do well as automotive technicians, I feel their talents are much more valuable as organizers and managers. Strong organizational and management skills are greatly lacking in the automotive industry and I am confident the ladies will be able to remedy this situation.

This leaves the important task of repairing automobiles up to the guys. Now guys, please don't think I'm turning my back on you. You see, I'm on your side too. If you think working on automobiles can be a little taxing, try dealing with the general public. Working with customers on a regular basis can be very emotionally draining. If you are burdened with periodic customer related issues then your mental capabilities will be greatly reduced for the diagnosis and repair of your customers' cars. I have said many times: "I wish there was a way a customer's vehicle could, by means of remote control, be delivered to the shop with a note on the steering wheel stating needed repairs". I have also said many times: "I know exactly how to fix the vehicle, now I have to figure out how to fix the customer!".

So guys, don't think you are getting the "short end of the stick" because I am recommending you should be positioned in the shop doing what appears to be the hard work while the ladies are handling the "cushy" office work. It "Just Ain't" so!! This said, guys, please be happy you are safely nestled in the shop area and at a safe distance from customers. Not to worry, the ladies can handle it just fine!!

So, the bottom line is this: *the guys, in most cases, will be much more suited for the repair of automobiles.* And, the *ladies, in most cases, will be most effective handling the administrative aspect of the business.* Please bear with me on this issue because we are striving for "Super Efficiency" and this is the best way I know to achieve this important goal.

Neatness

Although the ladies will most likely be responsible for the office activities, they are also going to be your shop "neatness police". To be sure, this also applies to your lady customers. When they enter the shop, there is a good chance the ladies will not make a single verbal comment about the condition of the shop area unless it's very neat and clean. Now, when they do enter the shop area and no comment is made, that could mean it's cleanup time.

You can get another important clue from observing body language when one of your lady customers is invited into the shop area for one of those occasional "show and tell" sessions. If they hesitate and kind of look around before walking through the shop area you may be well past cleanup time. If they refuse to enter the shop area then you are way, way past cleanup time. You need a serious "blow out" cleanup day! The careful observation of subtle input like this is what will help keep you on top of your game and ahead of your competition. Whether the communication is verbal or nonverbal, pay close attention to what the ladies are trying to tell you. They really want to help.

Please note: throughout this guide I try to reinforce the very important point that you must have insurance that allows for occasional escorted customer visits into the shop area. The "hands on", "show and tell" technique which is discussed in a later section is critical to customer relations. This approach is also very important for customer confidence but if you don't have adequate insurance to accommodate this occasional event please do not allow customers into the shop area. One mishap and you are out of business. No one wants that!

The Service Advisor

I have discovered that a really great candidate for this position is an ASE certified automotive technician who, for whatever reason, chooses to work in an office setting as opposed to a shop environment. I started working in the reception and service advising area of my business because I was experiencing difficulties with my hands. The extended exposure to harsh chemicals and frequent washing almost destroyed the skin on my hands. Keep in mind this was before the days of warnings about these damaging chemicals so no one wore protective gloves.

An applicant could have also had a job related injury or could have developed a disability while working as a technician. In either case, they could be great candidates for a service writing position. The advantage is they will be extremely knowledgeable in the repair of automobiles. This is extremely beneficial when explaining details of repairs to customers.

The only down side to an individual with these qualifications is they may give out too much information. Remember, you are in the business of repairing automobiles, not giving people advice on how to fix their own automobiles. Now, to be sure, there have been times when I gave out substantive information concerning the repair of a customer's vehicle. In most cases when this happened I was too busy to add to my workload. I also did it to help out a good customer who may have been a little short of funds and couldn't afford the repair. In either case, ninety-nine times out of a hundred, they came back and left their vehicle for repair. The important thing to remember is if you give out any information make absolutely certain it's to one of your very good customers.

We all know automobiles are so technologically advanced few individuals can perform their own repairs anyway. Quite often, if they attempted to repair their own automobile, they could do more harm than good which would most likely end up costing them even more money. So, be certain you advise your customer as to the possible pitfalls of doing their own repairs. But, be very cautious as to the information you give out. Giving free advice could cost you a customer and that's never good.

That said, having an ASE certified technician working as a service advisor is *Not* an absolute necessity. It is perfectly fine to have an individual who has service writing experience but has never worked on an automobile in their life. In reality you, the owner, will most likely be the service advisor even though you may or may not have automotive or automotive service advising experience.

This actually holds true for most individuals who are service advisors. They actually learned their trade from observations and discussions with certified automotive technicians. You can, with some effort, pick up this knowledge fairly quickly. Even though modern day cars are very complex, it actually will not take you very long to sound like a seasoned pro when discussing repairs with your customers.

In the beginning your work load will, in many instances, not be that great, in which case, your shop team leader will have time to interact with your customers and explain repairs. This is a tremendous benefit in that your customer will have the opportunity to bond with the person who will either be doing or supervising the repairs to their vehicle. In most cases a customer will bring their car in, drop it off, and then, as far as they know it enters a black hole. Having the new customer talk to your shop team leader will work wonders for perpetuating that "warm fuzzy" feeling and confidence in your shop.

If you are new to auto repair and choose to become a service advisor at your place of business, this is what I want you to do: while your shop team leader is discussing repairs with the customer you will stand silently and listen to the conversation. When your shop team leader speaks, look directly at him or her. When your customer speaks, look directly at him or her. Remain focused and listen to each and every word they say and file it in a safe place in your memory bank. Do this with each and every customer who comes to your repair facility. The discussions will be ever so slightly different with each encounter but this is how you will learn all of the different responses from your customers and your shop team leader. After a period of time you will have observed numerous customer and shop team leader discussions and been exposed to many different scenarios.

At this point, when the next shop team leader/customer encounter occurs and you get the urge to speak then, have at it. Feel free to become part of the conversation. You see, you are learning the automotive business and what a thrill it is. You are now participating in a process that will soon be all yours. Within a few short weeks you will have gone from knowing very little about an automobile to being somewhat of an authority.

With that said: a word of caution. Please don't think you "know it all" because automobiles are quite complex and there are many nuances associated with them. This is why you have a seasoned shop team leader close at hand. If you are not 110% confident as to your response to a customer's question then Stop!! Look your customer in the eye and say: "I don't know the answer to that question so I will let you speak with the shop team leader. He or she is the authority who can give you accurate information concerning your issue". Then, participate in the discussion so the next time this issue arises you will be confident with your answer. This will help free up your shop team leader to repair more vehicles and generate more revenue. The good news is, before long you will know all of the answers. Mission accomplished!

Keep in mind, the sooner you acquire this information the more efficient and self-sufficient you will be which will, in turn, add to your bottom line. In the early days of your business, your workload won't be that great so you will have a month or so to perfect your technique. Don't get complacent with this process because before you know it things will start to "pop". At this point, you will have to think fast and on your feet because customers and issues will be coming at you fast! It is important you treat this situation like a competitive sport. It is also important you get excited and energized when this happens.

Your energy and excitement will be detected by your customers and they will be very impressed as to how you perform under pressure. No matter what happens, do not curl under pressure. This will also be detected by your customers who will wonder if you are actually capable of repairing their vehicle efficiently, effectively and in a timely manner. You must always be confident and able to show that confidence.

At this point you may think I'm placing you under some pretty serious pressure and you would be exactly right. Remember, this is not a dress rehearsal, this is the real deal and rookie mistakes must be kept to a minimum. Keep in mind, this is quite a substantial investment for you and failure is not an option. Now for the good news: this doesn't last forever. Before you know it, the entire process will be second nature for you and answers and solutions will come to you with very little effort. At this point you may start to get bored with the routine and predictability and want to come up with creative ideas that will shake things up and get a little more excitement into your day. Fortunately most people are more comfortable with a nice routine so hopefully this will work better for you too. For sure, it makes it much easier to make money.

About now you may be thinking this is going to be way too much trouble. You may also say: "I don't know enough about automobiles, I'm not mechanically inclined, and I really don't want to take the time to acquire the necessary knowledge". The next logical thought is: "Maybe I should forget about the automotive business and do something else". Not so fast! This situation is not in any way, shape, or form a problem. The solution is as simple as acquiring a reliable, qualified shop and office staff and then, you become the General Manager. You see, some of the most successful people in the world had very little knowledge of the business they were in but had the ability to surround themselves with reliable, qualified individuals who had in-depth knowledge of the business. In reality this is the best case scenario because the primary problem in the automotive repair industry is poor business management practices.

If you are a strong business manager you are way ahead of the game. Everything you will need to know is in this guide so, in that respect, you have absolutely nothing to worry about. Business is business so if you have exact details of any given business then you can move seamlessly through the process and become quite successful. Above all, please don't get discouraged or have second thoughts because you will miss "the ride of your life" and we don't want that to happen. Success will be yours!

SECTION 5

Customer Considerations

Your Best Customers

This could be one of the most powerful business building techniques you will encounter in the auto repair industry. In many ways it's just plain old fashioned common sense but I will come out and say it anyway: *Cater to the Ladies*. And yes, you heard me right. According to current statistics, there are more single women than not, so this is a huge demographic. One of the reasons catering to the ladies is so important is, whether married or not, they tend to make the final decision on personal finances. When you have a situation where you have customers who are a couple, always listen to what the lady says! If you do this one very simple thing you will never go wrong. With all due respect, the lady may or may not completely understand all of the details of the repair (as with many guys) but she will definitely let you know if there will be sufficient funds to pay for the repair when it is completed. Women will admit up front if money is a problem whereas men won't. So, *Listen To the Ladies!!*

Another reason you should cater to the ladies is, historically they have been treated so poorly by the auto repair industry they just want to be able to take their car to an auto repair facility where they will be treated fairly and honestly. With this in mind, one of your primary goals will be to develop the trust of the ladies and be very honest with them. Remember, women are very good communicators and tend to talk amongst themselves and, therefore, can spread the good word about your repair shop. Keep in mind, the opposite occurrence can also happen. If you lose their trust, the word will spread like wildfire and you will be losing business at an alarming rate.

While they may or may not fully understand all of the details of the repairs (as with many guys) on their vehicle, the ladies will definitely know when you are trying to "pull the wool" over their eyes. If you ever attempt to be deceitful or dishonest with one of your lady customers (shame on you) and you start to feel guilty afterward, there is a very good reason. *She is already fully aware of your antics and you are not getting away with anything!!* One of two things will happen: either you will never see this customer again or, if she does return it's because you are, unfortunately, the least dishonest repair shop. She is only settling for your service until someone better comes along. I don't know about you but, under these circumstances, I would not be very proud of myself. Keep in mind, these ladies are going to be the very best, most reliable, long term customers you will ever have, so why would you ever consider treating them like anything other than your very best friend?

Once you've earned this new customer's trust it's time to go the extra mile. Now it's time to pull out all of the stops and prove to this individual they came to the right place to have their vehicle repaired. This is when the personal, hands-on approach is most beneficial and when the customer will be able to view all old, defective parts and get to see the new replacement parts. In addition, they will also get a complete explanation of necessary repairs. In other words, a very productive "show and tell" session. For sure, the ladies (and guys) will always enjoy and appreciate your extra time and effort.

Always explain a repair to a lady exactly the same way you would explain it to a guy. Don't attempt to "dumb down" an explanation for the ladies because you think they won't understand what's going on. They understand far more about a vehicle than you would ever imagine. Out of necessity, they have done their homework with regards to the repair of their vehicle so feel free to explain away in whatever terms you feel necessary to convey the message. If they happen to not quite understand a certain aspect of a repair, explain it from a different approach but *don't do it in a condescending manner:* no one wants to feel as though you think they are stupid. There are many highly intelligent individuals, both guys and ladies, who have no idea how an automobile operates and that's fine. You are the automotive expert so if you really want this person to be included as one of your really great customers then you will have to come up with a good, logical and intelligent method of explaining the repair. Trust me, you will think of something very creative.

If the trust issue remains in place, the ladies will rarely if ever contradict your findings or plan of action. In other words, they will rarely act like a "know it all" and that's what makes the hands on, show and tell session so productive. *Less debate, more action.* Within a matter of minutes with clear, concise communication, the repair will be under way and their vehicle will soon be completed and heading to the "finished line" ready for pick up. I think you will agree this is a very nice arrangement.

Communicating With Your Customers

I think we can all agree, effective customer communication is key to operating a profitable automotive business. Good communication can make the difference between having a great day and having a horrible day. The good news: effective communication is actually fairly easy but it does require some effort on your part.

The most important aspect of communication is to ***Assume Nothing.*** Your customers may know very little or quite a bit about automobiles but you must explain the repair and the associated costs to all customers using the same detail and terminology. If you take the time to explain all details you will never have a problem with the customer coming back saying: "You didn't tell me you were going to do that!".

Repetition is one of the best ways to convey a message. The old expression of: "Tell them what you are going to tell them, then tell them, and then tell them what you just told them" works every time. This technique will also help *you* remember what *you* said so *you* can remind the customer of what *you* said in conversation if a disagreement arises.

It is also very important for you to remember what the customer said during the discussion so the conversation can be reconstructed at a later date should the need arise. This process may seem a little time consuming but wait until you fail to communicate something and see how much time that takes!

One of the best communication techniques which works quite well is the "*Hands On*" approach. If you recall, I have mentioned this very important concept at various locations in this guide. This is when you actually take the customer into the shop area and place your hand on the defective part, and say: "This is the part that must be replaced." and then, explain the reason for replacement. Of course, you can only use this technique if your garage owners insurance allows for customers in the shop area. Your insurance company will most likely require your accompaniment while the customer is in the work area but that will be the case anyway.

This process will give you much credibility because it will be extremely clear to the customer your business is very transparent. You will not be hiding anything! It will also give your customer the opportunity to experience your clean, well-organized shop area. Once you are certain the customer understands the repair you should usher them out as quickly as possible to limit their exposure to any potential hazards and allow the tech to move forward with the repair. At this point, your valued customer is satisfied they are getting the correct repair so they can get on with their life and have one less worry. Customer comfort is very important and this is one more method of achieving this goal.

Accurate and precise communication is most important when your customer brings their car in for repair. If the problems with a car are not communicated properly the correct diagnosis will be all but impossible. Customers will make statements about the problems with their car as though they know exactly what they are talking about. In almost every case they won't have a clue as to what is wrong with their vehicle. Most of their information came from "helpful" friends who also don't have a clue as to what's going on. Now, you have two clueless people trying to tell you what to do. You are the seasoned automotive professional so it's your job to get to the bottom of this issue. Here are some simple methods to accomplish this important task.

First: you need symptoms from the customer: *not a diagnosis.* All you have to do is ask these simple questions: (1) What is your car doing? And (2) What are the symptoms? Now you are going to get data you can work with. In almost every case you will discover the repair will actually be much different from what the customer originally asked for. Do not forget these questions! You will be asking these same questions of every customer who walks through your door.

Even if they request something as simple as a tune up, you will still ask for symptoms because they may think the tune up is going to fix a problem. The customer will rarely, if ever, be correct with their diagnosis but you must always be accurate with your diagnosis. You will not gain customer confidence by performing needless repairs just to figure out the actual problem later. Precise diagnosis will be one of your primary objectives so asking the right questions will help you achieve this goal.

The second step for determining what is wrong with a vehicle is to *take a ten minute road test with the customer in their car.* Let the customer do the driving because they may have a unique driving style that will help duplicate the problem. If you hear a sound or feel anything unusual make sure you ask the customer if that is what they heard or felt. Many vehicles have multiple issues but the customer, for whatever reason, doesn't consider them problems. You want to make sure you are focused on the correct sound or feel so the diagnosis and repair will be correct. Once in the shop, it may take a while to locate the source of the problem but you can at least be confident you are concentrating on the symptoms for the problem the customer is most concerned with.

These are two very important steps that must be adhered to without fail. In order to have a successful repair facility it must operate like a well-oiled machine. Asking the correct questions and doing a thorough road test are the two steps for achieving this goal. Customers will also be very impressed with your concern for their vehicle and your analytical abilities. They have most likely never experienced this kind of attention at any other auto repair shop so you have now achieved a level of respect and credibility that places you head and shoulders above the competition. You have accomplished several objectives at the same time. Not only did you very efficiently and effectively communicate and diagnose a (possibly) complex problem with their vehicle, but you also secured them as a lifelong customer who will recommend you to everyone they know. These steps may take a little extra time up front but your long term rewards will be immense. It is details like this that will set you apart from all other competitors in your field.

To summarize this important concept: always remember to ask the questions: "What is your car doing?" and "What are the symptoms?". Also, do not forget the thorough road test to confirm the correct symptoms. With these two simple steps you or your techs can quickly and easily diagnose and repair problems with a car so you can move on to the next. More cars repaired more quickly equals more cash flow and that's how you make money.

The next extremely important phase of communications with your customers occurs when the car enters the shop. As soon as the diagnosis is complete it is time to calculate the estimated cost of repairs. ***This is a step that can never be ignored!*** Your customer most likely told you when they dropped their car off at your shop; "I trust your judgment so go ahead and repair my car. You don't have to call me with an estimate".

Ignore Those Statements! You Will contact each and every customer with an estimate of repairs!! Once again, every customer will get an estimate of repairs and *must also give authorization before repairs begin!*

You may have known the customer for years and think you have them figured out but under no circumstances are you to perform any repairs on their car without authorization. This is one of the best ways I know of to lose a loyal, longtime customer. They may have done some research online and tried to diagnose their problem and determine what the cost should be. The problem may or may not be what they thought it was and the bill might be twice what they had figured. Your really great customer will most likely come in, pick their car up, pay for the repair and not say anything to you. You may think everything is fine but your customer is now experiencing some doubt. Now, keep in mind, if this happens not only have you created doubt in that customers mind but they will convey this to their friends. At this point, not only are you about to lose one customer, you could be losing more and you will never know how many.

Doing an estimate is important but can be tricky. We all know anything can happen when working on an automobile. Sometimes there are tell-tale signs that will let you know problems may occur. Rust and corrosion top this list but there are many others. Some are highly visible but many of the other problems are not. Whenever you are making an estimate for a repair you must always add time to the flat rate (computer) manual time.

For those individuals who are not familiar with the concept of "flat rate time" I should explain how this works. Flat rate time refers to the amount of time allowed to perform a certain "operation" or component replacement on any given vehicle. All flat rate times were originally determined by the manufacturer of a specific new automobile. The method they use is fairly simple and straightforward. The times are determined by a team of technicians removing and replacing the same part on the same vehicle. The same operation is performed three consecutive times on the same make and model of vehicle. An average time is calculated for each attempt by averaging each team member's time. Now, this is the amount of time that will appear in flat rate manuals and computer programs.

The major flaw with this system is they use new cars to determine the times but, in the real world these repairs will never be performed on brand new cars. By the time these repairs are required the car may have been in service for some years. So, we are back to the rust, corrosion and other unknowns of repairing the car. My general rule was to add approximately twenty five percent to the flat rate time but feel free to use your best judgement with regard to this issue This would generally cover the time necessary to perform the repair. With that said, when you call a customer with an estimate for repairs you must make it very clear this price is based on the repair going as planned. Explain that problems can arise at any time. In many cases other problems will occur during the process of performing the repair. You could discover one or more failing components or bolts may be stuck or could break, etc. As I mentioned before, anything can happen! The customer *Must* be informed and fully understand these issues prior to giving the final go ahead for the repairs.

Once you have the customer's authorization, the repairs can be started. The parts show up and they appear to be correct so the technician starts working on the car. You will be making rounds periodically to check on progress with vehicles being repaired. Once a vehicle has reached a point where the area needing repair has been disassembled and with all parts cleaned, inspected and ready for reassembly, you are going to contact the customer. You will let them know that: "So far the repair is going fine and their car should be completed on schedule".

You should realize your customer is most likely at work trying to perform their duties and, at the same time, worrying about how their car repair is going. By making this very important phone call you took a huge burden off of them so now they can get back to being a hundred percent focused on their job. What a relief for your customer! If they thought you were the best before, they will really love you now!

Progress reports are one of the most important services you can provide your customers. The previous scenario of a repair going well is preferred but the opposite situation can and often does occur. Your tech comes up to you and says, "Boss, I'm having a problem with this car: a bolt just broke". Now, the critical phone call must be made. As soon as problems occur and a new cost to repair is determined the customer must be contacted immediately. In some cases, you won't be able to give a firm estimate because the outcome is quite often uncertain. These calls are never any fun but they are an absolute necessity. In most cases it isn't as bad as you might think. Remember, when you gave the customer the estimate you made sure they understood something could go wrong. If they do get a little combative all you have to is politely refresh their memory of the discussion you had when the car was dropped off for repairs. Remind them of the potential pitfalls of repairing cars that have some age and mileage on them and let them know you are doing everything possible to get back on track with the repair and trying to keep costs as low as possible.

As I will discuss in more detail in the following section, this is not the same situation as a customer complaint when you are to remain silent and let the customer do all of the talking. By all means, let the customer talk as much as they feel is necessary to communicate their thoughts but you should inject your thoughts periodically too. Politely answer all questions as clearly and precisely as possible. If you feel as though oral communications are not adequate, then by all means, invite the customer to the shop for a "hands on" session and see if that works better. Have a "show and tell" session whereby the customer can see and touch the actual part or parts that will require replacement. At the same time, you should also give a clear explanation as to why the repair is necessary.

If this is one of your many good regular customers it is extremely important that you put your best foot forward and *absorb a portion of the cost of the additional work*. If you have been following the advice of this guide you will most assuredly have the excess funds available to accommodate occasional occurrences like this. This is one of the best repeat and referral business building principles I know of so please don't ignore this advice! The only possible exception is, if the car is a total piece of junk you should have advised the customer to get rid of the car as opposed to repairing. So, you can see this is a judgment call with some variables. Once again, if this is one of your really great customers and they have other vehicles they bring in on a regular basis for repairs then I would say absorb a portion of the expense and move on. The bottom line is to ask yourself the question: "How much revenue does this customer generate for me in a year's time?", then make your decision.

When the repair is done, the thorough road test is complete and all is well with the car we have one more thing to do. You and the owner of the car are a little frazzled by now so a happy ending would truly be icing on the cake. What you are going to do now is wash and clean the car inside and out. It should look so nice the customer won't be able to recognize it. Once they have paid for the repair and go out to get in their car they will come back into the office and announce: "I can't find my car! There is one out there that looks like mine but it looks brand new!". At this point you know you've done your job. Once again, your customer will love you even more and will share their experience with everyone.

In summary: it is very important to stay in close contact with your customers and give regular progress reports while their car is being repaired. Be sure to make these calls when the repair is going well and especially when they are not going well. The customer must know the status of their vehicle at all times and without having to initiate the call. This is a very important concept to remember in order to retain and build your customer base.

Last: "When the going gets tough the tough must get going!". When you encounter the occasional problem vehicle then you must dig your heels in and do the right thing. Give in and absorb some of the cost of the repair. Go above and beyond the call of duty by cleaning their car inside and out. You will be way ahead of the game because customer loyalty and referrals should rank high on the list as one of your primary goals.

Customer Relations

Rule number one is: *never argue with a customer!!* With that said, the concept of, "the customer is always right" is seriously flawed. This next statement may sound a little confusing but is very true. *The customer may not always be right but they are never wrong!* If you argue with the customer you will most likely lose that customer. I will repeat, if *you argue you lose!* Now, you will most likely ask yourself: "If the customer is not always right but I can't argue with them, how is that going to work?". Well, this is how:

As mentioned in the section on your private, soundproof office: if you have a customer complaint then you and the customer are to go straight there to handle the matter. You can sit or stand but sitting is preferred. Make sure you and the customer are assuming the same position. Looking eye to eye and at the same level is very important.

At this point you will let the customer do all of the talking. They will most likely give you an ear full but you should never interrupt. Look them in the eye and nod from time to time to let them know you are paying attention: which you will be. Allow them to continue to talk until they have said everything that is on their mind and then they will stop. At this point, you will look them in the eye and say: "Tell me what you think I should do to make this right?". You have now completely and totally disarmed the customer but, at the same time, you may be thinking you just got yourself in a position whereby you may have to write this customer a blank check. Instead, when the customer responds you will be shocked and amazed to find out how little they will ask of you.

Most of the problem with the customer was they were frustrated because, when they have taken their car to other repair shops, they have received the run around and are sure you will do the same. Never do that! Face off with the problem and fix it. The customer let you off easy so now is your chance to shine.

At this point, *you fix the problem* and *you fix it right*. It's your job to make this your personal project. Never delegate this to anyone else. If you are a non-technician owner or manager then you will very strictly supervise and manage the technician who will be working on this vehicle. Your customer will identify the fact you are working hard to keep their business and, as a result, will remain loyal.

As icing on the cake, they will recommend you to their friends which will, in turn, add substantially to your customer base. All of this happened because you were the bigger person and chose to remain calm and to not argue with your customer. The customer pays your salary so keeping them happy better be one of your highest priorities!

In my shop, whenever a customer had an issue with a repair on their vehicle they would first ask for me. That was good! Next, I would determine which technician performed the repairs on the particular vehicle. Then, I had them accompany me when I discussed the issue with the customer. With the repair order in hand and the technician standing next to me, I would introduce the customer to the technician and let them know this was the person who made the repairs to their car. I would have the customer explain the problem to the technician and, at that point, it was the technician's responsibility to explain to the customer what, why and how they made the repairs to their vehicle. By observing body language, I could tell if the technician had done the repairs properly and by the book or had possibly attempted a little short cut. Needless to say, a couple of trips to the "hot seat" made the technicians a bit more conscientious and dramatically reduced customer related issues. Funny how that works!

Now that I've scared you by talking about customer complaints, there's a little known concept as it relates to customers that I would like to share with you. Hopefully this will ease your mind a bit. The best way to explain this is to consider your entire customer base. Some math will be required so let's say for explanation purposes your customer base is 100 percent. Now let me break this 100 percent down into the individual categories.

We will start with the easy one. Most of your customers will be in the 90 percent group. These individuals will be your very best customers. They will be more than happy to pay a fair price for good service and not complain. All you have to do is the same thing you do every day: diagnose the problem, communicate the problem, repair the problem, charge a fair price and they will be happy. These will be customers you can count on through thick and thin and they will be there when you need them the most. When you open your doors every morning they will be there front and center knowing you will be looking out for their best interest.

Now for the next group of customers. These customers will be your "great" five percent group. They will also be excellent customers. These customers are very nice and very good people who are very easy to please. The only issue with them is sometimes they will tell you everything is fine when it really isn't. It is important you are able to read body language and to listen carefully to their choice of words. There will be clues something is wrong and it's your job to ask the right questions and get to the truth so the issue can be resolved. These customers rarely complain but they do have a tendency to move on. The potential for losing them is quite high. Although they are a very small percentage, this group of customers is a great source for referrals so keeping them happy is very beneficial. Keep in mind, referral business is your very best business. These referred customers walk in the door trusting you because, if their friends think you are trustworthy then you must be.

Now for the final five percent. These are the customers who will drive you NUTS!!! You will never be able to satisfy this group of people! They will fuss and complain about everything you do. They will try to get you to shortcut a repair or try to get you to reduce the cost of the repair. No matter what you do they will never be happy! Do not waste your valuable time on these people! They will constantly want to argue with you and, as I stated previously, you will not participate in an argument with these customers or any other customer for that matter! If you lower yourself by getting into a debate with them you will end up just as miserable as they are. Now you've really lost!! It is crucial that you identify these people as soon as possible and direct them to another repair facility. They must GO!!

The very best approach is to listen to what they have to say and this time when they finally stop talking, instead of asking what you can do to make this right, say: "I'm sorry you feel that way but it appears as though I won't be able to do anything for you. You should take your vehicle somewhere else. I'm sure they can fix the problem better than I can. Have a nice day".

At this point, you walk away and end the conversation. If they continue to argue then feel free to have them removed by local law enforcement. These people must leave your property and never come back!!! They will truly suck the life out of you and your business! You don't have to worry about loss to your customer base because most of their friends are just like they are so you are better off without them. In addition, their normal friends know what kind of person they are and, as a result, will ignore their comments. You will most likely be a little nervous using this tactic but don't worry: it works. Good News: you have now freed up the extra time you need to focus on your very important 95 percent customer base!!! Whew: all this said, it's time to move on!

SECTION 6

The Professional Shop Team

Now, it's time to talk about your professional shop team. I am referring to the guys and ladies who will be working in the shop area and whose job it is to quickly, efficiently and professionally repair your customers' cars. These are the seasoned professional team members who are going to make you look really great in the eyes of your customers. Your job is to be the fearless leader who will be guiding these special individuals to keep them working as a team and moving in a forward, positive direction. To be sure, this is one of the most important topics that will be covered in this guide so please pay close attention. If you do not have at least a reasonably qualified shop staff that is willing to work as a team, and under your direction, you may have to rethink this entire process.

First of all, let's talk about you: the owner. Whether you are positioned in the shop or the office, your shop staff will behave exactly as you behave. If you act as though you don't care then they won't care. If you have a negative attitude they will also have a negative attitude. If you are unshaven, not well kept and poorly dressed then your staff will be unshaven, not well kept and poorly dressed. If you choose to use profanity and other off color language so will your shop staff. As a side note: Remember, your focus is on attracting lady customers so a poor use of words can really cost you in your all-important "Lady Powered" customer base.

To be sure, you must be the perfect role model for your shop staff (and office staff). You must command their respect at all times. You must be their "Fearless Leader", always making good and fair decisions under all circumstances. You must be consistent in how you manage and operate. This way you can be predictable and, as a result, your staff can start making some routine decisions on their own. You may think this could be a little risky but remember you've been setting a good example for them so they will be returning the favor.

My most rewarding days were those days when I had to step out to take care of a few business matters or to have a casual "Thank You" lunch with one of my really great customers. I could easily do this on a regular basis because I never worried about problems going unresolved in my absence. When I returned to the shop and asked: "So, did everything go all right while I was gone?". They would always reply: "Well, a few things happened but we remembered what you did the last time this same problem came up and that's what we did". Of course, I thanked them for watching my back and then I would jokingly remark: "One of these days they wouldn't need me to make any more decisions because they could handle it!". Their response was always a unanimous: "Boss, please don't do that: even though we did exactly what we knew you would do, it still made us very nervous".

Now, to be sure, the word "Boss" was strictly a term of endearment and I took it as quite the compliment. You see, if I had behaved like the "Big Bossy Boss" they would have been too intimidated to nickname me "Boss". You should never elevate yourself above those who you work with. One of the best ways to lose respect from your shop team is to develop a superiority complex. I always made it a point when I introduced one of my staff members that I never made reference to the fact they were an *employee* or mentioned they worked *For* me. I was always careful to mention they worked *With* me. Always remember, it is perfectly fine to be "one of the guys" when it comes to your shop staff. Everyone knows you are the owner so there is no need to hold it over their heads. If you expect your shop staff to behave like equal team members then you must behave like an equal team member. The concept of, "do as I say, not as I do" never works.

You should make it a point to connect with your shop staff on a personal level. I'm not talking about prying into their lives but, instead, ask general questions as to how their families are doing. If they have mentioned one of their elderly parents is not doing well then a simple, "How is your mother (or father) doing?" will go a long way to let them know you care: and you will. If they have a son or daughter who is doing well in school simply ask and give them a chance to brag. If you care about your shop staff then they will care about you. A word of caution, if you are not sincere they will know so, don't say it if you don't mean it!

Another good morale booster is to pick a day and do an extended lunch for the entire shop team. From time to time your work load will level off so you won't be killing yourselves to keep up and you can take the opportunity to relax and reflect. Announce the event a day in advance so no one will bring their lunch and have it go to waste. Ask your team to vote on what they want to eat so the food will be suitable for everyone. When we did this, even though lunch was treated more like a social event than a business gathering, it seemed as though everybody wanted to talk about work. The topics seemed to always gravitate to things that went wrong but that was actually good. This would give the guys an opportunity to boast a little about how they were faced with a problem car and how they analyzed and resolved the issue. They had their day in the sun with the added benefit of, the other techs learned from their problem solving adventure. The beauty of the whole process was everyone was having fun.

To summarize this concept: you must be a person your shop staff will respect and look up to for guidance and direction. Remember they will behave exactly as you behave so be extremely cautious as to what you say and do. Its fine to be friends with your shop staff and it is very important you take a sincere interest in their personal lives by responding to them when they talk about their family or about projects they are doing at home. Whether you are discussing business or personal matters, always be sincere and honest.

Okay, before I start discussing how to acquire and build your shop team there is one topic you, the shop owner, must understand and take to heart before you enter into this business. First and foremost, the day you open your doors for business you probably won't have any customers. The first week you are in business you will have a few customers. The first month you are in business you will have a few more customers. As you may guess, it's going to be a while before you develop a decent work load. You may well be the "Chief Cook and Bottle Washer": at least for a while.

In the beginning, the farthest thing from your mind is building a shop staff. You will have your hands full with your daily tasks. For sure, you will be able to repair your customer's cars: that's a given. If you have been repairing automobiles for some years, that's going to be the easy part. Try to not stress when working on customers cars since it will negatively affect your performance. You must keep your mind clear and focused for what might be very new to you: running an auto repair business.

The most important thing you can do is read and study the concepts in this guide and make them second nature. Remember, I have already made all of the mistakes so you won't have to. You may look at all of the details in this guide and wonder what difference they will make. Well, I promise you, if it's in this guide, it does make a difference. This endeavor is going to require your undivided attention so remember to focus, focus, focus! You are now on a mission and failure is not an option. Successful people never consider failure therefore you will never consider failure. Now, let's develop your shop team!

Developing Your Shop Team

There is so much material to cover regarding the development of your shop team, it's actually difficult to decide where to start. Have no fear, I promise to give you all of the necessary information you will need to develop your shop team and will present it in order of importance. I know you don't have the rest of your life to read this guide and start your business so I will make every effort to be factual and precise with the information so you can move forward to your goals.

Rule Number One: Hire Shop Team Members Who are Presently Employed

There is entirely too much auto repair work out there for any qualified automotive technician to not be working. There are a few legitimate excuses for a qualified tech being out of a job but they are rare.

Anything can happen so it is extremely important for you to do your homework when an applicant shows up who is not employed. There are exceptions so make sure you get all of the details and then verify. You definitely don't want to miss out on that special team member.

I can quote a personal situation whereby I was seeking employment and wasn't working at the time. I had been working at a very large factory owned dealership and due to some serious ethics issues, made the decision to quit. I witnessed corruption and dishonesty on a daily basis that would absolutely boggle the mind. I discussed the issue with the top management of the dealership and soon realized they were the source of the problem so I got the heck out of there. Even though I quit I made the decision to not let this issue go unnoticed. I contacted the corporate office which was located in another state and was fortunate to get in contact with the right person. They informed me of their suspicions of corruption at that dealership but they didn't have sufficient proof of this activity but now they did. They thanked me for contacting them and, long story short, the dealership was closed within a week.

As a result of this closing seven of my best friends and co-workers lost their jobs. Although more shop staff lost their jobs, these guys were the best of the best and at the top of their game. They were suddenly unemployed but through no fault of their own. They all had families and responsibilities and were in no position to lose their jobs. I was sure they would be upset with me but, to my amazement, they thanked me. The reason they didn't do the same thing I did was the fear of losing their jobs and not being able to provide for their families.

One of my many theories on life is that: if something falls through it just means something better is coming along. Well, it held true. Within days of the old dealership closing we were all working at new jobs with higher pay and better benefits. We were actually getting flooded with calls from area dealerships and repair facilities who wanted us to come to work for them. You see, we were fortunate in that the news of the closing of the dealership and the reason for closing was broadcast on the local television stations so almost everyone in the area was aware of what had happened.

I know I promised you I would not waste your time with a lot of boring or insignificant details but I have several reasons for telling this story. The primary reason is to illustrate the fact, in business, there are many situations that require judgment calls. If I had said: "Hire shop team members who are presently employed" and not qualified that statement with more explanation, you might miss out on a highly qualified shop team member. This would have been a great disservice to you and to the highly qualified individual who could not figure out why you said "No" to them. You must ask all of the right questions, do your research, and above all, think on your feet.

Rule Number Two: Applicant Must be Neat With a Good Personality and Attitude

Auto mechanics have in the past displayed a less than stellar performance in these areas. It was a given that anyone who worked on automobiles was generally dirty, poorly dressed, grumpy, and were very poor communicators. These are precisely the characteristics we do not want in shop team members. Fortunately, "the times they are a-changin' ". The term "mechanic" has pretty much fallen by the wayside and the term "technician" has taken its place. Thank goodness, with this designation a higher personal standard has finally emerged. Let's talk about what you should be looking for in an auto service professional (technician).

Neatness

It goes without saying, you want a sharp looking group of team members in your shop work area. As I have mentioned, you will be escorting customers into the shop area from time to time to discuss repairs. If you remember the discussion we had about the appearance of the shop: it should be spotless and well organized and this also applies to your shop team members. If someone applies for a position as one of your shop team members they should at least be moderately well dressed and groomed. You see, if they look a little disheveled when applying for a job imagine how they will look when they start to work with you. I'm actually giving them the benefit of the doubt because if they were planning on applying for job at my shop they better have a really good reason for not being neat and clean. Having someone apply for a position at your shop who is dirty and poorly dressed is very disrespectful to you and at the same time may be delivering a message. There is a chance your shop doesn't have the reputation for being the cleanest facility in town so this could be your clue you have some work on your hands! On the other hand, if you are starting out then the word of your "clean shop" hasn't had a chance to spread.

Now, you might think: "If they may have been working on cars all day then they will most likely not be neat and clean". My response in this case would be: they are most definitely not working at the right shop. When I had my repair shop people constantly commented on how clean the technicians in the shop appeared. Their question was generally: "How can they work on dirty old cars all day and not get dirty?". My response was: "Well, that's easy, they don't work on dirty old cars because we clean them first!". To be sure, this concept of auto technicians being dirty at the end of the work day must come to an end!

Personality

As a reminder, they (we) are not "mechanics" anymore, they (we) are "technicians". To go a step further, when these technicians come on board with you, their title will then be elevated to shop team member. Personality is extremely important for the all-important team concept to work. Customers will also be coming into contact with your shop team members from time to time so the theme of "making a good impression" must prevail. Your shop team members must have the ability to smile, speak clearly and have a good command of the English language. The use of any profanity is strictly prohibited. You see, one of our primary goals is to give our customers that warm fuzzy feeling from the time they drop their car off until the time they pick it up. In most cases the customer gets that warm and fuzzy feeling when they leave their car but as they discover more about the inner workings of the operation that feeling soon disappears. You will not let this happen!

Now, with this said, personality is not a deal killer. In many cases you will encounter very qualified technicians applying for a position at your shop who are good people but may not be displaying those really strong personality traits you want to see. Please keep in mind, these individuals could very well be your most knowledgeable and most qualified candidates.

For the record, I was one of those guys with the "not so great personality" but, thank goodness there were enough people who could see past it and allow me to progress in the automotive profession. Keep in mind, when most individuals are exposed to people with the more desirable, outgoing personality characteristics they tend to take on these same traits. That's what happened in my case. Remember, the most important take away from this discussion is this: *make certain you attract the most qualified technicians and the personality issue will take care of itself.*

So, this is what you will be doing: seeing past little flaws so you can develop a great overall shop team. I guess that's really the name of the game anyway isn't it? No one is perfect so this is simply another one of the judgment calls you will have to make.

Attitude

I just mentioned: "Team member personality was important but not a real deal killer!". *Well, attitude, and specifically a bad attitude associated with negative thinking, is most definitely a* ***Deal Killer.*** Under no circumstances are you to permit any individual with negative thinking and/or a bad attitude to ever be employed in your establishment: and, this applies to any job!! All you need is one person on the team with a bad attitude and, who thinks and speaks negatively and before you know it you will no longer have a team. A team member with a bad attitude is exactly like a terminal illness in that, sooner or later, they are going to do you in. You and your other team members may have the best attitudes and could be the most positive thinkers on the planet but one person with a bad attitude can bring all that crashing down. In the long run you and your positive team members will certainly win out over these individuals but why waste your valuable time? Remember, you and your "winning team" have vehicles to repair and money to make.

Rule Number Three: Applicant Must Have a Well-Equipped Tool Box

Make sure one of your earliest discussions with a potential team member addresses the status of their tools. It goes without saying, tools are an absolute necessity if you plan on repairing automobiles. To be clear, I'm not talking about a junky old tool box filled with "cow" tools; I'm talking about nice high quality tools in a decent tool box. Of course, some of the very best techs out there don't have the shiniest new tools in the shiniest new tool boxes but that could be one of your best clues as to how good they are. I believe: "It isn't what you've got, it's what you can do with what you've got". This is so very true when it comes to automotive tools. If a technician truly knows what they are doing they will know exactly what tools they need and will not clutter their tool box with tools they don't need. If you recall, back in the section on shop organization, I mentioned those wonderful "Aircraft Carrier" tool boxes that all of the techs are buying. I also mentioned the fact they take up a lot of your valuable floor space. If your techs have smaller, well-equipped tool boxes that will be to your benefit.

You may have an applicant tell you all of their tools were recently stolen. Now, I'm not going to sit (stand) here and say their tools weren't stolen, I'm just saying it sounds like somebody's trying to "pull the wool" over your eyes. They either didn't have tools to begin with, or they had to sell them to pay some bills. In either case this applicant probably isn't going to be of any benefit to shop productivity. But, once again, do your homework: this person could be a pearl in disguise! You will be faced with many judgment calls and this could be another one of them.

Possibly this little success story will give you some insight into this particular situation. This happened a good while back at my repair shop. We were getting consistently overloaded with work and having problems hitting our deadlines so it was time to add a shop team member. I put the word out and started getting some decent responses. Most of the applicants seemed to be well qualified and I was in the process of doing my homework and deciding who I would be bringing on board. Then, on the day I was going to make my decision, another applicant showed up at my door. He was neatly dressed, clean cut, very personable and spoke very well. Now, imagine my confusion when he told me he wasn't presently employed and had to sell his tools to pay bills. Well this decision was going to be easy to make, right? Wrong! Let me explain.

Based on his neat, clean and personable presentation, I knew there had to be a back story and I was determined to get to the bottom of it and quick. He made the job very easy for me with his willingness to share the details of his situation. He had a young daughter who was suffering from a health related abnormality that was diagnosed at birth. The health insurance he had at his previous employer had maxed out and, as a result, were refusing to continue coverage for her. Hospital and other bills were mounting up so he made the decision to sell his tools with the hopes he could find another line of work to earn income. Now he had two problems. First, finding another line of work that would pay a decent salary and second, repairing automobiles is a passion for really good technicians and given a little time to think about it he realized auto repair was what he really wanted to do.

The following is the story of how this event played out. Although this story deviates from the current subject, there is a lot of valuable business related information embedded in this segment so please read and pay close attention to the details. You may be faced with a similar situation so this information may give you some insight that will help you arrive at a suitable solution.

Okay. Now, I had my work cut out for me. I instantly got on the phone to check references because this ball had to get rolling and now. I checked out all of his references and everything came back positive. I had a very long chat with his previous employer who described him as the model employee and an excellent technician. He explained he had to let the guy go because, if he didn't have any tools, he couldn't work on cars and therefore would be of no benefit. Now it was solution time and I really had to kick into high gear! I love solving problems so this was right up my alley. To my amazement, the solutions that appeared to be very complex and convoluted were actually quite easy.

I called the guy back to ask him to come in and mentioned I needed more details of his situation. Within the hour he was in my office. We had two things to figure out: one, how could we resolve the issue of no tools, and two, how to figure out a really good solution to the problem of no health insurance for his daughter. To start with we had to fix the tool problem and get him to work. I was really getting behind on a few jobs and he really needed the income. When I asked him about the status of his tools he explained he had sold them lock, stock and barrel to his favorite tool route guy who just happened to be my favorite tool guy too. How convenient!

I immediately got on the phone with our tool guy to find out the status of the tools sold to him. He told me he had been very busy and he hadn't had time to do anything with them. As a result, they were still intact and on his truck. He was fully aware of the dilemma my new technician applicant was facing and the purpose of buying the tools was to help him out. He explained the situation the guy was in bothered him very much but he didn't know what else he could do. We talked for a few minutes longer as to how we could make something work and then he suddenly said; "I'll be there in twenty minutes with his tools!". I replied: "We have to know what kind of money we are looking at, so we can make a decision". He just said: "Don't worry about it, we'll figure it out".

Long story short, our tool guy figured several different scenarios and you will never guess what happened. It was getting close to the end of the year and, after a little number crunching session with his accountant, our favorite tool guy determined that if he wrote the tools off as a loss he would be about a thousand dollars ahead of the game after taxes. The end result: my new tech was working that very same day with his own tools and moving out some jobs that were in dire need of completion.

The tools were one problem down and we still had one to go. A little girl needed some good medical care and health insurance so she could get well and lead a normal life. That should have been easy enough. I belonged to a rather large automotive aftermarket association that had an agreement with a well-known and reputable health insurance company so all I had to do was sign my new team member up, add his family to the policy and we would be done. One problem! The insurance company had a special exception on certain pre-existing conditions; especially cases that had previously exceeded a certain cost with a prior insurance company.

I immediately got on the phone with the president of our automotive aftermarket association concerning the matter. Upon explaining the situation to him, he emphatically announced the insurance company response was grossly inaccurate and was definitely not going to fly. The agreement the association had with the insurance company stated all applicants would be accepted and covered regardless of any pre-existing issues. That sounded fairly straightforward to me!

Now it was time for my association president to contact the insurance company and refresh their memory as to the agreement they had signed. We immediately contacted the insurance company regional representative so we could quickly clear this matter up and move on. The representative was very polite and personable when he announced he didn't recall an agreement with our association and they had no record of one. He then apologized profusely for not being able to insure the little girl because, as he stated, her case was outside their guidelines so we were out of luck. Then he hung up the phone.

I believe most everyone is familiar with the story of David and Goliath. This could be my interpretation but, as the story goes, most looked at Goliath and thought he was way too big to hit, but little David looked at Goliath and said; "You know what, he's too big to miss!". So, David seized the moment and took his little slingshot and popped big Mr. Goliath and put him on the ground. Long story short, David found Goliath's weakness and took advantage of it. That's what we did with the insurance company.

As a general rule, if you go through the normal channels to resolve an issue and that doesn't work, go straight to Mr. Big. Clearly, we had exhausted the normal channels so it was on to the CEO of the insurance company. We quickly and easily located the CEO's name, address and contact information. The most efficient action was a simple call to the CEO, explaining the situation and hopefully resolving the issue. You can most likely guess how that went; the CEO was not accessible and the receptionist couldn't say when he would be available. When asked what the problem was we took great care in explaining the details of the situation. The receptionist assured us the CEO didn't handle issues like that and we should go back to our region manager for some kind of resolution. You could say that we "hit a big ole' stone wall".

But, we weren't done yet. There are advantages to being a member of a decently sized automotive aftermarket association. The president of the auto aftermarket association was well connected with the owner of several large metropolitan TV stations. These TV stations had excellent news divisions and happened to be looking for personal interest stories to help boost their ratings. I guess you can see where this is going. The owner of the TV stations decided to make a little friendly call to the CEO of the insurance company and, of course, he promptly got through. The owner of the TV stations told the CEO his insurance company was denying a little six year old girl health insurance and one of the stations just happened to have a copy of the footage they planned to air the next day concerning the case. To be polite, he was checking to see if the CEO wanted to make any comments before they put it on the evening news. It was a very one sided conversation and the CEO finally got the message Loud and Clear!!

We got our call from the CEO of the insurance company and he was prepared to resolve the issue. To insure this situation never came up again, the president of the auto aftermarket association and me along with the association attorney, hopped into the car and made the two and a half hour trip to the insurance company headquarters to have a sit down meeting. We, of course, had the original agreement that had been made with the insurance company and the wording was actually quite clear. The rules had changed but, thanks to our agreement, we were locked in. The little girl had her health insurance, and our mission was accomplished.

I really got off track this time but there is a lot of really valuable and important information embedded in this story. One lesson we can all learn from this is the really smart and compassionate decision our favorite tool guy made to write the tools off as opposed to selling them back for a profit. You see, if he had earned that extra profit by selling the tools, he would have placed himself in a higher tax bracket and it's hard to say how much money he would have lost. In addition, he would have greatly and negatively altered the future of a very valuable technician and his daughter. So, Thanks: nice move!!

The other very important message is: *Join Your Automotive Aftermarket Association as soon as possible*! There is nothing like strength in numbers when you have to get things done. Keep in mind, this entire sequence of events took place in about three days so a lot happened and it happened fast. This didn't occur by accident: it was a team effort. You would be amazed at what a group of motivated people can accomplish when they want to achieve a common goal. This is exactly how you want your auto repair business to function!

Rule Number Four: Applicant Must be Automotive Service Excellence (ASE) Certified

About now, the Automotive Service Excellence organization is most likely wondering why they weren't first on the list of qualifications. Good question! This is a wonderful organization that does an excellent job of organizing and providing technical training and testing materials for automotive technicians. Without ASE, automotive technicians would basically be on their own if they wanted to acquire advanced training. They could obtain training by other means but, historically, these alternative programs are not very well managed or structured.

Now, to answer ASE as to why they were not first on the list of qualifications: if an applicant is not currently employed, has a negative attitude, personality issues, or doesn't have adequate tools (and doesn't have a great explanation for all of these) then, regardless of training, qualifications, or certifications they would not be employed in my establishment.

Any technician who plans on being one of your shop team members ***Must*** be ASE certified. Keep in mind, a doctor can't be a doctor until they have all of the appropriate training, pass all of the tests and complete their hands on experience. The same applies to an automotive technician: proper training, pass tests and on the job experience. Simply stated: an automotive technician ***Must*** possess a phenomenal amount of information to function efficiently in the task of repairing automobiles.

Now, before you have a nervous breakdown over the volume of knowledge your techs must possess, let me explain a very important concept. I just stated, a good automotive technician must possess a tremendous amount of knowledge in order to be proficient in their trade. With that said, always remember: "It's not as important to possess knowledge as it is to know where to find this knowledge". You and your techs don't have to know everything about every car on the road but you do have to know where to find the information. Now granted, you will most likely not be working on every single make and model of vehicle but it wouldn't hurt to at least have the information available. There are several very good computer based programs on the market that are loaded with tons of data which will give you the information you need to repair almost any automobile you chose to work on. But, as discussed in a later section, it is very beneficial to specialize and not work on every vehicle that comes to your door. Specialization dramatically improves efficiency which in turn increases productivity and profits.

Always remember: all of your applicants must be ASE certified, although not necessarily in all categories and not at all levels. This is fine! The fact they are putting forth the effort counts for a lot. Should you decide to add them as a team member it will be your responsibility to make sure they continue on the path to full certification. Keep in mind, it is very important that your shop team leader or one of your team members is certified in all areas. In all fairness to your customers, if they are paying the going rate for service they deserve to have certified and qualified team members making repairs to their vehicles. If you were in their shoes you would expect the same. ASE certification, whether partial or full, is an absolute necessity. The ASE organization can easily be accessed online and they will be more than happy to assist qualified individuals with attaining their certification goals.

This is just my opinion but I believe rendering a service for which you are not qualified would come under the heading of "fraudulent behavior". Your shop team members must possess the appropriate training and the associated certificates if you wish to be a legitimate automotive repair facility that will be charging customers a fee for service. This simple concept applies to all businesses and is an absolute necessity for auto repair.

COMPENSATION: well it looks like I got this far discussing the acquisition of your shop team and have not mentioned how much your technicians should be compensated for their services at your repair facility. In other words: *How Much Should I Pay My Technicians*??

Excellent question!! Glad You Asked! Although this may seem like a very complex topic: it isn't. So, you will not have to worry about a lengthy dissertation. I like simple, direct and to the point so this is how I will handle this topic.

I think it comes as no surprise that different areas and regions have different costs of living so a technician's compensation or pay can vary greatly. Thank goodness for the internet the information related to these costs of living and associated salaries are readily available. Keep in mind, this information can experience some flaws in accuracy so I would consider this a starting point. Take care to check multiple sources to verify data. This is very important because your ability to attract the most qualified techs will be determined by what you are willing to pay. To be sure, it will be necessary to pay slightly MORE than the going rate if you want to attract the most productive shop team members. For sure, this will be a necessity but "not to worry" because these individuals are generally top performers so the added productivity should more than offset this additional expense.

Another excellent source for technician compensation data is from your shop team leader. Of course, in the very earliest stages of this process you will most likely not have a shop team leader. Since a highly qualified team leader will be your first priority I would, in the process of doing team leader interviews, simply ask them how much techs are being compensated in your area and they will generally tell you everything you need to know plus a little more. Naturally, if you are a technician/owner this information will be common knowledge for you.

As a "Best Business Practice" method of determining compensation, here is a guide line which I ***Strongly*** recommend you adhere to; *the compensation for your techs should be closely tied to your shop labor rate.* In other words, once you have done your market research and determined your competitive shop labor rate you can then determine what portion of that labor rate dollar will be available to compensate your technicians. Based on industry standard (and under normal conditions) approximately 20% to 25% of your total shop rate dollar should be available for technician compensation. To be sure, this includes *total compensation* which is *salary plus ALL bonuses and benefits*. This is a general rule but I think you will find this technique will adequately compensate your technicians, cover your overhead and also allow for a comfortable profit for you: the owner. This is a good starting point but, by all means run your own numbers and, if you feel the need, you can tweak these figures several percentage points up or down: just not too much!!

As far as pay structure is concerned, you will have several options. The primary technician pay structure for years has been "Straight Commission" but this is finally falling by the wayside. Thank Goodness!! This was a carry-over from the Great Depression era whereby people would work as needed and the business owners would pay them a percentage of the revenue they generated. This method pretty much disappeared many years ago for most industries but for some reason it held on for a long, long time in the automotive field. All I can tell you is this: you will *Never* acquire an effective shop team using this pay structure so it is a definite ***NO*** to "Straight Commission!!".

Now, if your plan is to run a well-managed, well-organized auto repair facility, this is my recommendation: *Using the 20% to 25% rule, pay your technicians a salary plus a performance bonus.* This is standard practice for most businesses but for the automotive industry is not that widely used. To be sure, this is by far the best way to develop a "high performance" shop team that will deliver the "goods" on a regular basis!! If your techs have to constantly worry with fluctuating pay checks they will have difficulty focusing on their work and, as a result, will not be as productive.

Of course, you will not be paying all of your techs the same salaries. Technician pay is a function of their level of ASE certification, experience and their ability to produce. Just so you know, some of your techs will be paid less than the recommended 20% and some will be paid more than the maximum of 25% but it should always average out. This is simply another judgement call on your part.

The good news as far as production is concerned, a basic shop management program can easily track the number of hours and the associated revenue which is generated by each tech so figuring productivity will not be that difficult. The beauty of this arrangement is you can do a weekly productivity report which will let each tech know if they are carrying their weight or not. This will serve as a nice little "wake up call" if they happen to not be delivering on the production end. And, if they did well: BONUS!!! So, it's a definite ***YES*** to the Salary plus Bonus method of compensation.

Okay: it's "Monkey Wrench Time!". If you recall, throughout this guide I have made mention of the possibility of a recession and/or economic down-turn while you are in the process of operating your auto repair business: it's a reality. And, I made mention of the fact you will have some judgement calls and adjustments to make.

That said, these guaranteed salaries plus bonuses which I just discussed may not be sustainable during a slowdown. So, you will need a backup plan if your desire is to weather the storm and come out the other end alive and well.

In this case you will have two options: (1) lay off several techs or, (2) Oh NO!! Straight Commission!! Please don't get upset with me for making this suggestion but, if the intention is for your business to survive, this could be a necessity: at least in the beginning.

To be absolutely clear on this matter: *this must be a prearranged agreement which you will have with your techs.* Now, to make this concept a bit more acceptable to your techs you can mention the other option which would be laying them off and let them (individually) make the decision. I think you will find that, under these circumstances, straight commission will be quite acceptable to all. Keep in mind, during a recession all of the other repair shops will be in the same boat (or much worse) so it's not as though your techs can go straight to another repair facility and get a job.

Sorry if this sounds a bit harsh but during a recession, belt tightening is everyone's responsibility: not just yours. *After all, you must remember you are in Business so these decisions must be made if you expect to thrive!!!*

Okay, it's time to move on!

SECTION 7

The Professional Business Team

Bookkeeper, Certified Public Accountant and Business Attorney

The information I am about to give you could be some of the most important advice you will receive in this entire guide. It is of utmost importance you have a team of professionals watching your finances. You may be well versed in the actual operation of an auto repair business but will most likely have minimal knowledge of bookkeeping, accounting and business law. The really great news is you don't have to because ***it's not your job***. You will have your hands full running your automotive business and will have little time to deal with these matters. What you will do is locate a good, honest and reliable bookkeeper, certified public accountant and an attorney who specializes in business law. Now you are covered.

You might think you can't afford to have these professionals when, in reality, you can't afford to not have these professionals. If you wait until you need the services of one of these individuals it may be too late. It is essential you have a good working relationship with each of these professionals prior to starting your business. Failure to heed this advice could cost you dearly in the long run so please don't ignore this information.

I just mentioned the fact you may be concerned about the expense of this professional team and are debating whether you really want to go this route. Allow me, at this time, to sell you on this concept.

Your bookkeeper, your accountant and your attorney all have automobiles and they make very good livings. Now, put the two together and where I come from you just acquired three very good customers. Moreover, these people are generally well connected and have many friends and associates who also have vehicles and make very decent livings. Now, all you have to do is make that great first impression and there is no telling how many magnificent customers you will acquire. Trust me, I made a lot more money off of my professional team than they ever made off of me. In addition to being really great customers, they can also help you make and save more money than you ever thought possible.

I will now give you a few guidelines to follow that will help you select your bookkeeper, accountant and business attorney. Since accountants and attorneys are licensed, the process is somewhat easier. In most cases, bookkeepers are generally not licensed but finding a good one is not very difficult either so, not to worry. Do your homework and you will easily be able to assemble an efficient and cost effective professional team.

Bookkeeper

To start, you are most likely thinking the concept of a bookkeeper is rather dated. You are probably thinking to yourself: there are lots of computer based bookkeeping programs out there that should serve my purpose fine. I don't know what your experience is with computer programs but, if I had a nickel for every time a computer program fouled up or fell short I would have a whole "truck full of nickels". As wonderful as computers are, they can never replace a human being. A person, unlike a computer, has experience and is capable of making decisions and judgment calls. Computer programs attempt to do this but, quite often, fail miserably. The human mind is more powerful than the most powerful computer ever developed so use your mind to its fullest extent and take advantage of the minds of others. Once your mind is turned on you can feel free to turn your computer on. If you direct a computer properly they can be a powerful and productive tool but a person must be in control.

Since bookkeepers are generally not licensed, the very most important first step is when a bookkeeper applies, get as many references as possible and then verify these references. This is a must-do step! Ignore this and you could have problems that will be difficult to correct: the very most important of which is the improper handling of tax related issues.

Of course your accountant also handles tax issues, but it's your bookkeeper's job to take care of monthly tax filing procedures and dates because failing to file appropriately could cost you big bucks in penalties and interest. These are taxes such as sales tax, withholding tax and other payroll related issues. Your accountant, in most cases, will be responsible for state and federal income taxes but will rarely deal with these monthly taxes. Some accountants actually offer bookkeeping services so if you find a good accountant then the bookkeeper will most likely also be good. As you can see, your bookkeeper has several very important tasks which must be performed in a very timely and professional manner. For this reason it is most important you select a highly qualified bookkeeper!

The good news: as far as a bookkeeper is concerned, they don't have to be full time. Most bookkeepers go from job to job and quite often work at each location no more than a few hours per week. It all depends on what needs to be done. These days there are really great shop management programs that track income and expenses and greatly reduce the need for a bookkeeper but don't think for one second you can do without one.

As soon as you get the notion to save a few dollars and do the bookkeeping yourself: Stop right there! If you have no bookkeeping experience or chose to hire an unqualified individual to handle the bookkeeping task you are headed for trouble. Honestly, you would almost be better off doing nothing as opposed to trying either of these options. Doing your own bookkeeping without any experience and/or allowing an unqualified person to do your bookkeeping is one of the most foolish business decisions you can make so please don't go there.

The exception to this comment is if you choose to take the position as general manager and you also have bookkeeping experience, then handling your own bookkeeping could be an option. As you likely already know, there are several really good computer bookkeeping programs on the market so definitely use one of those if you are comfortable with this arrangement. However, as mentioned earlier, these programs can be a bit glitchy. So still, human input would be quite beneficial and I would strongly recommend having a bookkeeper on-call on a consultation basis. All you have to do is miss a tax filing date and you will quickly see the benefit of having a qualified bookkeeper looking over your shoulder and giving guidance.

I should mention your bookkeeping method must be a function of what your certified public accountant recommends. It is essential your bookkeeping system flows seamlessly with your accountant's system. This will dramatically save you money and aggravation in the long run so please don't forget to coordinate this with your accountant.

This is very important: your bookkeeper is going to know a lot about you, both financially and personally. *Honesty* is an absolute necessity but *confidentiality* is equally important. The concept of "loose lips sink ships" holds true especially in the business sector. As I said before, bookkeepers go from business to business and location to location so they come in contact with lots of other business owners. You absolutely, positively do not want any of your business information to get into the hands of another business person: especially your competition!

The solution is quite simple: have your bookkeeper sign a *confidentiality agreement*. This can be as simple as a few sentences stating they are not to discuss any aspect of your business with any other person or entity without your written permission. I would also make mention of penalties for their failure to comply. This will greatly improve their memory should they have a weaker moment and accidentally want to say something to an unauthorized individual. You would be wise to consult with your attorney and follow their recommendations.

At this point you are most likely wondering if you will ever be able to get a bookkeeper if they are required to sign this confidentiality agreement. All well-managed businesses will have a confidentiality agreement with their bookkeeper and, for this reason, you will also have a confidentiality agreement with your bookkeeper. As I mentioned before, confidentiality is the accepted method of doing business so there should not be any hesitancy to sign. If a bookkeeper chooses to not sign the agreement that would constitute a huge red flag and, at that point, they would be disqualified for the position. Not to worry, you will find a wonderful and qualified bookkeeper. Always remember, references, references, references and then verify references. And, don't forget, your accountant could be a great resource for finding a good bookkeeper.

Certified Public Accountant

You will notice I said Certified Public Accountant, not just accountant. There is a fairly substantial difference. As you might guess the word "certified" means more qualified and more experience. Let's say it's like ASE certification for an automotive technician. Simply put, this means a person, whether accountant or automotive technician, has exerted the additional effort to excel in their field. Now, I'm not going to stand here and say an uncertified accountant is not as competent as a certified accountant; I'm just saying certification gives credibility. Certification is evidence they should be held to a higher standard but it is definitely not a guarantee of performance.

Now we are back to the concept of references, references, references and then verify references. You must understand, in any given profession, there are really great individuals and there are the not so great individuals. It goes without saying, this also holds true for accountants. As you may guess, we are "on the hunt" for the great accountant. In addition to locating a great accountant we want a great accountant with reasonable fees. To be sure, we are not looking for cheap but we are looking for fair. If you go to an accountant's office and it is super fancy with gold plated door knobs I would wave them off and keep searching. A super nice office or an average office, a certified public account is a certified public accountant. The credentials are the same: one accountant is a "show boat" while the other is a normal, conscientious, hard working person like we are. I'll go with the conscientious, hardworking accountant any day. Just my opinion but I think you will agree with me on this one. Simply stated: you don't have to pay an outrageous fee to get a great accountant.

If you are interviewing a potential accountant candidate and they start bragging as to all of the little tricks they pull to save people money on taxes then I would be suspicious. Some accountants will tell you this to get your business and, generally, individuals don't care for paying taxes so this strategy serves as a nice "hook" for most people. Quite honestly, the tax code allows for so many legitimate tax deductions and credits that I have no idea why anyone would consider doing anything dishonest. A qualified CPA can easily pick and choose from a grocery list of deductions and credits and advise you as to what will work best for you.

Very important: do not play games with taxes. That's about the best way I can think of to get into some seriously deep trouble and I am not kidding. If you have given your accountant all of the information he or she has requested and they arrive at a figure you owe for taxes, simply pay it. If you feel as though the amount is not correct then definitely question their figures. They could have made an honest mistake or possibly you failed to tell your accountant about a large piece of equipment you purchased which should have been depreciated. Once this is resolved to your satisfaction go ahead pay the taxes and move on.

Please don't let something like this make you bitter! The more you fuss, fret and agonize over paying these taxes, the longer it will take you to get back on track for making more money. The forward momentum must never be slowed. Got a little off subject again but this is important stuff.

I know I should be discussing your certified public account but, since we took a little detour talking about taxes, I would like to include a few more thoughts and then move on. I couldn't think of a better place to talk "taxes" and some of the legitimate tax deductions you can enjoy in the operation of your automotive business. I'm going to discuss a few of the tax deductions and tax credits that are available to you but, by all means, consult your CPA before doing anything. I have knowledge of these deductions but I am truly not the expert.

Just so we are on the same page, any and all expenses generated in the process of operating your business are tax deductible. In other words, gross receipts (the total amount of money you bring in) less total expenses equals' (before tax) net profit. This is approximately the amount you will be paying taxes on. Of course, other issues such as depreciation on equipment and charitable contributions will also reduce your tax liability. This is very basic but I think you get the idea.

Now I'm going to get a little more advanced with a particular and legitimate tax deduction. This comes with a word of warning: it is necessary you adhere to the letter of the law when you use this technique for a tax deduction. I'm giving you this information so you will have an example of what is possible and then you can make your own decisions based on your CPA's recommendations.

33 Ford Roadster at Factory 5 Racing, Wareham, MA.

Now, here is the example of a legitimate tax deduction which may come as a surprise to you. You are in the auto repair business because you absolutely love cars. It has been your dream for quite some time to build a really nice street rod but couldn't justify the expense. Well, here's your opportunity. You figure the project will cost you about twenty thousand dollars and decide it's worth the money and effort so you go for it.

First, you purchase a suitable vehicle. You then locate and purchase all of the necessary parts and materials and you go to work building your special street machine. You were very careful to keep all of your receipts, including all expenses required to transport the vehicle and all of the associated parts to your shop.

Since you are a determined goal oriented individual you were able to complete the project before the end of the year. When you painted your "Little Baby" you did a nice custom paint job which included a very creative graphic that included the name of your auto repair facility. Guess what you did. That's right, you just *created a twenty thousand dollar advertising expense* AND *got a sweet little hot rod to boot*!

Now, all you have to do is drive your little rolling advertisement around and it's legitimate. You can give your customers joy rides, participate in parades, cruise popular neighborhoods, or participate in car shows. You are advertising your business wherever the car goes and it's all tax deductible! Once again, when you do something like this, consult your CPA and follow the tax code to the letter and everything will be fine.

Without belaboring this subject, I think you get the idea of the range of possibilities as far as tax deductions are concerned. Your CPA can elaborate on other ideas so I will, now, keep quiet and let them do their job. I hope they don't get upset with me for giving you ideas but I wanted you to know at least one of the many perks you will be able to enjoy in the process of operating your automotive repair business.

Another valuable concept is that minority and woman owned businesses are given preferential treatment by the IRS and the government. The plan is to encourage more women and minorities to open businesses. I'm most certainly in favor of this concept. With a little help from Uncle Sam and this guide I hope to see many more women and minorities in the automotive business. Ask your accountant about these important benefits.

I think this gives you a fairly good overview for selecting a certified public accountant, what your expectations should be and some suggestions as to how you can legitimately reduce your tax liability.

Business Attorney

Last but not least: selecting your business attorney. To be sure, an attorney is an absolute necessity but, at the same time, you hope you will never need one. If you follow the recommendations in this guide it will essentially eliminate the need for an attorney but it would be nice to have one to consult: at least in the early days of your auto repair business. Make sure he or she is familiar with business law and is also a good trial lawyer.

You can be the "best of the best" and something could happen that could possibly end you up in court. If you recall in the section dedicated to customers I mentioned the five percent group who you can never satisfy. Well, if you happen to not identify them quickly enough you could be court bound and you definitely do not want their attorney to beat up your attorney. That would be a terrible shame since you will most likely be the victim in this case. In the event this occasion does arise be absolutely positive your attorney has plenty of courtroom experience.

Fees

I don't think you will have much luck finding an inexpensive attorney. They tend to keep fairly close track of what other attorneys are charging and they tend to stick together on their fees. That's the way it is and I think that's a common practice just about anywhere you go. I can't really say anything because a smart auto repair shop owner knows what his or her competition is charging and will adjust accordingly. I did it all the time so I know how it works.

Searching for a really good and reasonable attorney may well be out of the question so the best approach is to simply locate an attorney who is good. As mentioned, ***reasonable*** may be out of the question but I would still check around just in case there is one out there somewhere. Now all you have to do is ask around and you will hear certain names come up on a regular basis. If you hear the same name come up three or four times you may have found the right attorney for the job.

Oddly enough, another way to find the right attorney is to talk to several attorneys and they will recommend another attorney that will fill the bill perfectly. All attorneys had to pass the bar exam for the state in which they are practicing so they should all be competent.

It is very important that, when you finally decide on an attorney, make sure they are not too busy to respond when you need assistance. An attorney who does not respond is just as bad as not having an attorney at all so you must get some assurance they will respond upon request. Quite often attorneys will request a retainer for service in advance so this is when you make it quite clear; when you call for assistance they are to respond in a timely manner and with good, well thought out answers to your concerns. The attorney you selected can be the best and most competent attorney on the planet but if they are not responsive to your needs they are of no value to you.

Your attorney deserves respect from you but, at the same time, you deserve respect from your attorney. Never be intimidated by an attorney. If, at any time, you feel as though they are not being respectful to you by not responding quickly, giving you marginal information and/or not responsive to your needs then feel free to "fire them". Honestly, they are charging you a lot of money for their service so if they are not performing they must be replaced. Keep in mind, there are more where they came from! Even after you have made the initial decision on which attorney to go with, keep your ears open for other possibilities. Being in business and not having access to a good reliable attorney is not a good position to be in, so please don't allow yourself to get in to this situation.

Now we have our Professional Business Team in place. Your "***total business package***" is now complete. We started with the office/reception team whose primary goal is to cheerfully receive the customer, create that all important great first impression and then, make certain all of their automotive needs are facilitated in a timely and professional manner.

Next, we developed the shop team. Most importantly, the primary goal of the shop team is to generate the revenue that is the basis of the existence of your business. These are the highly skilled, professional automotive service technicians whose objectives are to accurately diagnose and repair customers' automobiles and deliver them in perfect working order. The goal of the shop team leader is to work in complete harmony with the shop team and the office team and keep the lines of communication open between the two.

Last but not least, we developed our professional business team. The primary goal of the professional business team is to make sure the revenue which is generated by the business is accounted for, distributed properly and that no one will try to take it from you. This will help you achieve your objective of maximizing net profit so you have more disposable income. I am willing to bet this is what you had in mind when you started this process.

SECTION 8

Business Considerations

General Auto Repair vs. Specialization

To be sure, there are many business strategies for auto repair facilities. To the average person observing an automotive operation it looks like the techs are simply working on cars but to the trained eye it's a whole different story. What the untrained eye cannot pick up on is *specialization.* Specialization is one of the greatest keys to success in the automotive business.

Of course, you can opt for a broad specialization or a more specific one. There are different schools of thought for either approach so this will be another one of your many judgment calls. There are many techs who feel more comfortable repairing specific makes and models but then, other techs enjoy the variety and challenge associated with working on many makes and models of vehicles.

Even though I originally specialized in the repair of popular imported vehicles, due to demand, I started repairing exotic makes and models and found it to be very exciting and invigorating. At that time I had repaired so many different and unusual makes and models of imported vehicles I really needed something that would give me a challenge. My motivation for working on exotics was to give myself a thrill which it did and the side-effect was I made a ton of money in the process. I guess the point I'm trying to make is this: your degree of specialization can be at any level but, if you are tired of your comfort zone feel free to advance to the next level.

The General Auto Repair Approach

General auto repair simply means you will do *any and all repairs to any and all vehicles* that show up at your doorstep. This approach basically describes the vast majority of auto repair facilities in existence today. This approach is the reason there are many auto repair facilities that are either barely making a living, or just making ends meet. Now, to be sure, there are a number of general auto repair shops that are doing quite well but I'm willing to bet it took them a while to get there. I am certain there was a great deal of trial and error along the way so it wasn't an easy process. My goal is to help you cut to the chase and avoid the trial and error phase of this process.

The general auto repair approach can be a struggle because of the lack of efficiency. Every vehicle you work on will be different and for each repair you will have to figure out a new game plan to get the job done. All of this takes valuable time. Even though your shop data program will provide you with the technical information, there are many specialized tools you will need. Many of the repairs will end up being a struggle with one issue after the other slowing you down. You will be striving to make your auto repair facility operate in a fluid and seamless manner and you can see this will make your goal more difficult to attain.

As an Important side note: Before I get too far, allow me to make an important clarification on the definition of "general auto repair". It is important to note the "any and all" repairs portion of that definition. It is perfectly fine to work on *all vehicles* that show up at your doorstep, it's just you will not be doing *all repairs* to these vehicles. Many very successful repair facilities work on about every vehicle that shows up but the difference is they only service one or two components on these vehicles. They could do transmissions, or brakes and exhaust, or tune up and maintenance service, or other specific components. Even though they work on all makes and models of vehicles, they are actually specialists. As you may guess, this can be quite lucrative.

The Specialized Auto Repair Approach

As you may guess, the *specialized approach* will be much different from the general approach. The specialized approach will greatly enhance your ability to achieve a fluid and seamless operation of your business. The advantages will be quite obvious from the start. As soon as a vehicle shows up at your shop and the customer starts to describe the symptoms, you will already have the problem diagnosed. Not only will you know what the problem is, there is a good chance you will have the part or parts in stock. If special tools are required there is a very good chance you will have them in the shop waiting for the repair.

I think you can begin to see the efficiency of the specialized approach. You will get to the point whereby you will not have to think about what you are doing. Your customer responses will be almost automatic in nature. This will make it much easier to schedule appointments and to let customers know in advance when their car will be ready for pick up. Estimates for repairs will be much easier because you will, most likely, have them memorized. You have the diagnosis, the parts, the tools and the know-how so you can see there's nothing to slow you down. Your confidence will also show which will be very impressive to your customers.

An important feature to stress with specialization is you will be able to keep most of the fast moving parts in stock. Because of the familiarity with your specialty you will know exactly which parts to keep in stock and approximately how many of those parts. The big advantage of stocking your own parts is you will be able to enjoy the benefits of quantity discounts. Instead of 50-100% markups you could be able to realize twice those amounts. Now you are making serious bonus money which will be substantially reflected in your bottom line. Keep in mind, this is the easy money you really didn't have to work for so that always helps. You will be charging fair market rates but you will also be generating more profit.

Another distinct advantage to specialization that is important to stress is the efficiency of repairs. The diagnosis will be quick and easy so that's out of the way. You have your hands on the part, or parts, and you are ready to rock and roll. If you recall, most estimates for repairs are based on "flat rate time" plus about twenty five percent which should easily compensate you. If you have performed this repair multiple times then it's a safe bet you will be able to beat standard flat rate time. If this does in fact happen you will make some pretty decent money. Now, if this is one of your really good customers I would highly suggest you deduct that twenty five percent cushion, or part of it, and save your customer some money. You made good money, you saved your customer some money and now you have reinforced your customer's loyalty which will ensure they will be back and with all their friends!

Final General vs. Specialized Considerations

Now that I have totally convinced you on the specialization approach, I'm going to slightly confuse matters and give a few arguments in favor of general auto repair. These are very important considerations you must be aware of before making the final, general versus specialized auto repair decision. This is an extremely important business decision so it is essential you get it right the first time. For sure, you can make adjustments along the way but that could dramatically slow you down on your path to achieving your goals. Here is a little more food for thought.

One argument in favor of the general auto repair approach is if your market area will not support a specialty. If, for whatever reason, you happen to select a rural or remote area to open your repair shop your location may not generate enough revenue from one or even several specialties. General auto repair will be your only option. At this point, you must consider yourself a highly skilled, versatile and talented technician because your work will definitely be cut out for you. The good news: many of your rural customers will be good, down to earth people who have little need for complicated vehicles so, from a technical standpoint, you should be in good shape. Their vehicles will most definitely need frequent repairs and the best part is they always seem to have the financial ability to pay for these repairs. Bottom line: if you locate in a rural or remote area, and you don't have data to suggest otherwise, general auto repair will be the way to go.

Another consideration with respect to general auto repair is the condition of the economy. Auto repair has a certain degree of recession resistance but is not immune to serious slowdowns. The slowdowns in auto repair generally occur in the earlier days of a recession but have a tendency to rebound substantially midway through and then remain strong for the duration of the recession. But, from the onset of a recession until that midway point, things could be a bit difficult for an auto repair facility that concentrates on one or even several specialties. For survival purposes you may be forced to take the route of general auto repair. Much worse things could happen: for instance, you could lose your business. Now that I put it that way, general auto repair isn't so bad after all now is it? Remember this business is your baby and you are definitely not going to let go of your baby.

If an economic downturn does occur and you have to revert to general auto repair, you should never feel like you are caving in on your master plan. This is the smart move to make and each day you delay making this adjustment the further you will fall behind your competition. This should be a prearranged event that should be clearly stated in your business plan. I worked for large, well-established dealerships that, when a recession was imminent, advertised they would work on any vehicle that could get through their doors. They did not want to be a casualty of a recession and neither do you.

If you read the "My Story" section in the beginning of this guide you will recall I started my auto repair business three days prior to the official announcement of a serious recession. Within two days I went from being an import car specialist to doing general auto repair. I decided I had to do what I had to do and the rest was history. I was bound and determined a recession was not going to kick my butt and I think you will agree you won't let it kick yours either.

This event did have a tremendous silver lining though: I learned more about auto repair in a six month period than I had learned in ten years. And, I thought I knew it all! It was truly a learning experience I will not soon forget. The moral to the story: if you believe in yourself and your auto repair business and you want that business to survive in a recession by all means take the general auto repair approach. You will be a better business person for it.

Here is another consideration for general auto repair. If you do happen to have a good size market area and your dream is to do general auto repair then, after all is said and done, I would say go for it. The smart way to do this is to specialize first, reach a level of competency and then branch out into another specialty. Keep this up until you feel as though you can accommodate all vehicles. I honestly think you will find if you did your market research your specialty will keep you quite busy so there would be little need to branch out into other areas.

One motivation for branching out into another specialty is if you want to expand and you feel as though your present specialty will not support your desired growth. In this case, by all means, branch out to gain the extra market share that will be necessary to support your expansion plans. Instead of going directly into general repair I would select another specialty that will complement your present specialty. As I mentioned before, once you have perfected your present specialty advancing to a new specialty will be a normal progression for your business. You already have the customer base so now you can offer additional services which they will really appreciate.

Back to specialization: I know I have been trying to make a few points in favor of general auto repair but I hope I have made even better arguments in favor of specialization. At the expense of sounding like a broken record, specialization is the preferred approach if your goal is making lots of money with your auto repair business. Selecting your specialty will be a very important task so here are a few guidelines that will help you with this very important aspect of your planning phase.

You must do a thorough market study before you make the decision as to what specialty you will pursue and the scope of that specialty. If your market study indicates the demand for your service will be marginal you really don't want to restrict yourself to that specialty. Remember, the idea here is to make money. At this point you will have to tweak your specialty to accommodate the needs of your market.

This is how I would determine a specialty or, depending on the market area, several specialties. Market needs are different for different areas so you will have to do a little leg and phone work to make your final decision. Your leg work involves going to all of the other automotive shops in your area and analyzing exactly what they are doing. Of course, you will be doing this at a distance since you will most likely be driving by. Keep in mind, while doing this, you are going to be your own private detective: as in, being rather "stealthy" and keeping a low profile.

That said, here is a technique that works well for the ladies. You can always drive right up to their place of business and play the part of a "Damsel in Distress" who is lost and needs directions. Once you get in the door of their place of business you can now make your own observations and draw your own conclusions as to how their business operates. At the same time, and with a certain degree of innocence, you can ask the questions: "So, what kind of repairs do you do here?" and "If I happen to need some work on my car, how long would it take for me to get an appointment?".

Now, at this point, you may think this technique is a little underhanded but it's *NOT!* Remember, this is business! *ALL* well-managed businesses know exactly what their competition is doing and how they are doing it so, have at it and check out your competition.

The information you gather through this process will give you a general idea as to what they are doing, how they are doing it and if they are busy. I would strongly suggest future "drive by" visits to see if the same cars are still hanging around. In many cases a repair shop can look busy but, in reality, they are not. The point I want to make is this: a bunch of vehicles on their lot and in the shop does not necessarily mean they are busy. These vehicles must be repaired and delivered in order to make money.

Of course, if they are members of your auto aftermarket association (which I'm sure you promptly joined) you can simply walk right in and the owner will most likely tell you anything you want to know about their operation. As you may guess, this is by far the easiest way to gather market data!

Another excellent method of getting information from your competition, that is, if they are not association members, is to give them a call as though you are a potential customer. Ask them some questions about the details of their services. Ask what they do or don't do. Also, be sure to ask how much they charge for their different services. Once again, ask the all-important question: "If I decide to bring my car in for repair, how long will it be before I can get an appointment?". This is the important question because the answer will let you know how busy they really are. If they have appointments scheduled for a week or more that's a fairly good clue this service is in demand.

Another approach to this technique: I'm sure you have friends with cars and those cars have some issues but they are waiting for you to open your facility to get the repairs done. Simply have them visit all of the repair shops in the area to get estimates, opinions and any other information they can acquire. Have them make written and mental notes and then have them report to you. With the exception of your personal visit, this is one of the very best ways for acquiring information on your competition. By the way, if you are feeling the least bit guilty: Don't! If your competition is taking care of business as they should they will be doing the same thing to you once you open your auto repair business. This will be an ongoing technique you will be using on a regular basis for as long as you are in business. Keep in mind, the point of this technique is *you always want to know what your competition is doing so you can do it better.*

In the final analysis: the most important thing to remember is specialization first and, when all else fails, go the route of general auto repair. Specialization will dramatically streamline the auto repair process which will allow your auto repair facility to function more efficiently which will, in turn, generate more revenue.

On the other hand, general auto repair will be somewhat more problematic. Efficiency and productivity will be reduced due to the lack of familiarity with all of the different automotive product lines. Diagnosis will be much more time consuming. It will be difficult and expensive to have all of the specialized tools to make the repairs on the many and varied vehicles you will encounter on a daily basis. It will also be difficult to stock all of the fast moving parts necessary to service the multiple makes and models of vehicles.

There are several good reasons to take the general auto repair approach. One reason is, if your market area will not support a specialty or even several specialties. Another very good reason to go the general repair route would be in cases of a recession or economic hard times. General repairs may be the only way you will be able to keep enough cars in your shop to turn a decent profit. An additional argument for doing general repairs is if that's what you really want to do. After all, it's your repair facility so who am I to tell you what to do with your business! I'm simply giving you my best advice but, at the end of the day, the decision is all yours. I have the utmost confidence you will make all of the right decisions and choices for your auto repair shop.

What's In A Name

I cannot over emphasize the importance of creating an effective name or "brand" for your automotive business. I guess you can say, the name of your business is basically a really great marketing tool. Okay, I'll just come out and say it: *"The name you give your auto repair business is a really, really great marketing tool!"*. Your business name is your personal "brand" which customers, and potential customers, will be able to easily recognize and identify. It is very important your business name strikes a "responsive chord" with your customers, and potential customers, in a way that will appeal to their emotions. Now, time for some effective guidelines for naming your business which will give you that all important edge you will want and need in the auto repair industry.

Although my goal is to give you lots of suggestions for properly naming your business, I think it is very important I let you know of a few things you should *Never Do*. You see, the name of your business can have a positive effect, neutral effect or, possibly, a negative effect for acquiring customers. We really want to avoid the neutral or negative routes at all costs.

Number One *Don't Do*: *Never ever, ever use initials or groups of letters to name your business.* Now, to be sure, there are many, many businesses with groups of letters forming their name and I suppose they have a good reason for doing it that way. A good friend of mine named his business using the first letter of each of his children's names. Understandably, this was very important to him so, in this case, it was justified. The name didn't help his business any but it helped him work harder because he was dedicated to his family. In this case, had he selected a nice informative "feel good" name, it may well have served him and his family better by generating more business, more income and would have done it more efficiently.

I will never question the motivation of any other business owners taking this route; it's just if you want a nice positive "feel good" informative name, using letters or initials will definitely *Not work!*

I would also try to avoid names that use a person's first name and then "Auto Repair". No creativity here and besides that, doesn't this person have a last name. Lots of people have the same first name but a last name would more accurately identify them. I will address this scenario in detail later in this section.

Another big "Never Do" is any off-color, derogatory or confusing, meaningless names. You may think this is common sense, and I would agree, but you still see some business names and have to say "What?". It's almost as though these people want to self-destruct before they get started but maybe they think the name is cute. Unfortunately nobody else will. I won't bother giving any examples of these names but I think you know what I'm talking about.

As a side note: I have seen some very creative names for businesses that didn't make sense at first but, once I realized what the message was, I never forgot. The point I want to make is this: feel free to be creative but don't be so creative the average individual won't catch on fairly quickly. *Creative – Yes: Complicated - No.*

Figuring out the perfect name is really not as easy as you may think. A shorter business name is easy to remember but a longer name gives you the opportunity to convey more of a message or emotion. Yep! We are back to the most powerful marketing tool of all: *Emotion.* Later in this guide, I mention in the section on "Advertising and Marketing" *emphasizing emotion is far more important than stressing facts.* Well, this also applies to your business name. Looks like we figured out a really great technique for reducing the size of your business name. Concentrate on *emotion* and the *facts* will take care of themselves. Believe me, this is a proven technique.

Happy, positive words are what we are looking for. There are so many words that fit this description I wouldn't know where to start. If I started giving you examples of some really good business names I would most likely squelch your imagination and creativity and that would be a terrible thing for me to do.

WOW! I just had a pleasant "light bulb" moment. This is a perfect time for the lady, or ladies, to kick into high gear. Imagination and creativity are their forte so who better to tackle this very important undertaking. As you may recall, we are trying to attract lady customers so who would be better at naming a business that would attract a female clientele. Looks like the guys are off the hook for now but that just means you will have some extra time to tackle other tasks.

Another method for naming a business is to use your full name and then a three or four word "tag line" that describes your specialty or focus area. This is the method I used to name my automotive business. My business name was my full name and then: "Sports and Imports". Fairly simple and straightforward but it gave the customer two pieces of very important information. The business name stated (1) who I was and (2) what I did. Granted, there was no emotion involved but, since I included my first and last name in the business name, it meant I wasn't trying to hide the fact I was the owner of the business from my customers. If a customer had any issues with the operation of my business they knew exactly who to ask for and that was the way I liked it!

As a side note: Quite often businesses have customer complaints and the owner may never have knowledge of these issues. The customer most likely assumes the person working in the office is the owner so customer complaints never get to the actual owner and that could be very bad for business. I can tell you from experience that including your full name in your business name is a very bold move. But, it's a bold move that has immense benefits for your business and works wonders for customer comfort. The down side is you have to address all customer complaint issues but better to take care of these situations sooner than later. You really don't want to be out with your family eating dinner and have a dissatisfied customer give you an ear full. Awkward!

Here is a "tidbit" of information that is worthy of repeating. I know it's a little off subject but it's definitely worthy of mention. This is a brief explanation for why it's important the customer knows who the owner is. Since I have been touching on the subject of customer related issues throughout this guide, allow me to share a very effective technique which will dramatically reduce customer complaint problems. It's actually quite simple and effective. I mentioned it earlier in this guide but I feel, due to its importance, it is worth repeating.

In my repair shop whenever a customer had an issue with a repair on their vehicle they would first ask for me. That was good! Next, I would determine which technician performed the repairs on the particular vehicle. Then, I had them accompany me when I discussed the issue with the customer. With the repair order in hand and the technician standing next to me, I would introduce the customer to the technician and let them know this was the person who made the repairs to their car. I would have the customer explain the problem to the technician and, at that point, it was the technician's responsibility to explain to the customer what, why and how they made the repairs to their vehicle. By observing body language I could tell if the technician had performed the repairs properly and by the book or had possibly attempted a little short cut. Needless to say, a couple of trips to the "hot seat" made the technicians a bit more conscientious and dramatically reduced customer related issues. Funny how that works.

Once again, I got a little off track but I hope you can see the importance of this information. When I feel two or more concepts are related I want to show you the connection so this will all make sense. It's the little details that add up to big details. Everyone can see the big details but sometimes the little ones get lost in the "shuffle", so I will take every opportunity I have to emphasize these very important points.

Okay, back to naming your business. One of the latest and most effective techniques for naming an automotive business is to indicate you are very up to date, top of your game and technologically advanced etc. As complex as newer automobiles have become, "tag lines" that make reference to these characteristics are real attention grabbers for potential customers. Most customers look under the hood of their automobile and cannot imagine how anyone could have the skill and the knowledge to repair their car. If the name of your business indicates you are well versed in the latest technology your customer will be more comfortable that you will be competent to repair their complex, state of the art vehicle.

As a word of caution, *if you are going to represent yourself as technologically advanced* then *you better be technologically advanced.* It would be very dishonest to lead potential customers to believe you are up to date and knowledgeable when your repair shop has out of date equipment and worn out tools. The point I want to make is this: if you think you are not going to be able to live up to a "high tech" name then don't use this technique to name your business.

Keep in mind, the name you assign to your business will most likely be the name it will have for the duration of its life so this is something you really want to get right the first time. Granted, if you have been in business for a while and, for whatever reason, your business name is not working for you then, by all means change it!

If you happen to currently be in business and you think a name change is in order, I have a few suggestions. If you recall, earlier in this guide, I mentioned if you get comments and/or feedback from your customers it may be time to make some changes. Well, this also applies to your business name. If enough of your customers make the same or similar comments about your business name it's time to put your thinking cap on and try something different. I should mention you now have a great resource for coming up with a new name: *Your Customers*. If you asked your customers they would be more than happy to assist with this task. Since they didn't like your original name, they have most likely decided on a new name that would be more suitable for your business. Actually, customers enjoy contributing to your business because they really want you to succeed so you will be there for them when their vehicle needs its next repair. After all, your customers are paying your salary so anything that will keep them coming back should work perfectly for you.

A name change can be a bit complex from a business standpoint and could also be a little confusing to your really good repeat customers but, if you feel the name change will improve business over the "long haul", then go for it.

I know you have seen this with other businesses when they advertise. You will hear them make an announcement to the effect: "We are happy to announce to our many very loyal customers we will be changing our name. The only thing that will be changing is the name. We will continue to offer the same great service you have experienced in years past. The staff will remain the same so the same friendly faces will be greeting you on your next visit. See you soon!".

To be sure, there have been many well-established companies that have been in business for quite a few years that have changed their name. In every case, the change was designed to keep up with the times. This is a case where a name change was one of the best techniques they could use to improve business. When their business was started many years before the concept of including imagination, creativity and emotion in a business name was never a consideration and now these are the primary considerations. You see, customers associate old fashion business names with old fashion business practices. Granted, there are people out there who feel that's good but the vast majority of customers nowadays favor current, up to date, progressive businesses. This is especially important for auto repair because, if you are not current and up to date with technology, you are out of business: Period!

I bet you never thought in a million years naming your auto repair business would be so complex. I am a firm believer in *simpler is better*. Even though all of this information appears to be complicated, it really isn't. You may spend many hours and many brainstorming sessions and nothing will happen. The point I want to make is this: feel free to stress and agonize over your business name. This is perfectly normal! Then, out of nowhere the right name for your auto repair facility will come to you in such a magical fashion it will be hard to believe. Take my word for it, this is how the very best business names were, and are, developed.

No matter what you do, don't settle for a name. You want a name that will make you and your customers happy every time you, or they say it. Believe in your heart and in your mind the right name will come to you and when it does "Oh what a thrill!".

Business Structures

Before I begin recommending business structures, allow me to alert you to a business arrangement in which I strongly suggest you never participate. It's called a *partnership. I would never participate in a partnership with anyone!!* You may think you know a person fairly well and, under normal circumstances, you get along fine. To be sure, partnerships have destroyed more families, friendships and perfectly wonderful relationships than anyone could ever count. I could write a book on this one subject alone but I will spare you the gory details. It would take entirely too long, plus you really don't want to know. Please, take my word for it and move on.

Before I start discussing business structures, I feel it is necessary that I make it quite clear that I am most certainly not an attorney or an accountant. The overall information in this section is factual but could vary from state to state so always seek qualified legal counsel and a certified public accountant in your area before entering into any kind of business arrangement. My objective is to give you a brief overview of these business structures so you will have a basis for making your decisions.

Sole Proprietor

This simply means an individual went to the business license office in their area and purchased a business license. It's very easy and anyone can do it. This is by far the easiest way to go into business. All you have to do is fill out a form, pay an initial fee and you are in business.

To be sure, *this is another very undesirable business structure in which you should **never** participate!* I call this the "hood ornament" business structure because the hood ornament on a car is one of the first things to take a hit in an accident. A sole proprietorship is most assuredly an accident waiting to happen.

Allow me to clarify: in a sole proprietorship the business owner and the business are the same legal entity. If a mishap or a lawsuit occurs on a business level the sole proprietor is held personally liable for any monetary award. This means with a sole proprietorship you are now in a position to lose everything you've worked for all of your life. I'm talking about your house, your savings, your vehicles, your furniture, everything. If you guessed this situation would not be good, you would be exactly right!

Now, if I gave you a few minutes to think about it you may say: "Not to worry, I'll get insurance for that". The major flaw in this plan is sometimes insurance companies use technicalities to avoid paying a claim or the claim could exceed the limits of the policy. If I give you a few more minutes to think about it you might say: "Well, I'll just be careful and nothing will happen". Unfortunately, things you can do wrong are only half of the problem.

I am referring to situations which are out of your control. You see, there will be people on your property who will be there for various reasons but you, the owner, will be held personally responsible for the safety and wellbeing of these individuals regardless of why they are there. There could be a random pedestrian merely walking on your property and you are still responsible. You may or may not be aware of this but there are a fair number of people in all walks of life who are completely unable to "walk and chew gum" at the same time without injuring themselves. And yet, they have a perfect right to try to sue you for whatever amount they so desire.

I could go on for days with this subject but I think you get the message. At the expense of repeating myself, if you choose to go the route of sole proprietor you will be nothing more than a "hood ornament" guaranteed to get (personally) hit hard with the first mishap that comes your way. *This is no way to start or run a business so it's a definite* ***"No"*** *to Sole Proprietorship!!* Not to worry, the next business structure which I have been leading up to should be the solution you have been looking for!

Limited Liability Company

A Limited Liability Company (LLC) has most, if not all, of the benefits of a corporation. Something that I hope should be jumping out at you is the "Limited Liability" wording in the name of this business structure. I don't know about you but I kind of like the way that sounds. After all, we are in the business of making money, not giving it all away, so this arrangement could be quite beneficial. Allow me to elaborate.

The LLC business structure is actually a fairly recent development for the business community. The sole proprietor and corporation business structures have; however, been around forever and ever. The primary reason the LLC was developed was to accommodate startup and small businesses. If you wanted to go into business you basically had two choices, (1) sole proprietor and (2) corporation. The sole proprietor arrangement is very inexpensive but offers zero protection from a lawsuit. The corporation, on the other hand, can be fairly expensive, requires several company officers which you may not want and yearly paperwork filing, but offers excellent protection.

As you may guess, the vast majority of startups and small businesses would opt for a sole proprietorship because of the reduced expense but fail to acknowledge the extreme exposure to personal risk. Effective risk management is an important part of managing the day to day operation of your business. My question is: "Who on earth would put themselves in the position of earning a nice income just to have someone come along and take it away from them?". The answer is *No One!* As a result of this dilemma, the decision was made to create a business entity that allows one person to own it, is inexpensive and easy to form while, at the same time, offering good protection from personal risk. As a result, the LLC business structure was born.

The good news is an LLC is only slightly more difficult to form than a sole proprietorship. The process is relatively fast and inexpensive. Remember, you are also getting that all important protection from personal liability. About now I bet you are liking the way this all sounds but in the back of your mind you are thinking: "What's the catch?" and there isn't any catch. You see, government may have its problems but it also has its benefits. It is important to understand the economy must expand and grow if our nation is to continue to succeed. Although big business appears to have all of the wealth and power small business is the engine that powers the economy and moves us forward so it's easy to see why small business must prevail.

Prior to the formation of the LLC business structure many small business owners were voicing their concern over the fact a sole proprietorship did not provide any protection from personal risk. And, if they had to endure the expense and red tape of forming a corporation they might reconsider the wisdom of going into business. This situation would surely create a huge impact on the economy. So, thanks to the swift action of some key individuals and the formation of the LLC business structure, we now have an affordable method of going into business with the added assurance personal risk will be dramatically reduced. This is great news for all small business owners!

Now we can move on to the details for the formation of an LLC. Once again, it is very important I stress the fact I am, in no way shape or form, an authority on creating an LLC business structure. I have formed a number of LLC's, so I am going to describe the process for my state but it varies from state to state. As I have mentioned before, always consult your accountant or attorney for professional advice and direction.

To start: the formation of an LLC in my particular state is handled by our State Corporation Commission (SCC). In your state this agency could have a different name so take care to locate and confirm the appropriate agency that handles LLCs.

Step One

The first thing you must do is come up with a name for your business. This process was discussed in detail earlier so please refer to that section if you have any questions. You will not be able to register an LLC if you do not have a name for your business! As a matter of fact you may want to be prepared with several names in case your first and second choices of names are already reserved. You must contact the appropriate state agency directly by going on line or by phone to confirm the availability of a name. Two LLCs with the same name are not permitted so, if someone else has the name you like, you are out of luck. It's strictly a first come, first served arrangement.

With this fact fresh in your mind it is extremely important that, when you decide on a name, you contact the appropriate state agency immediately and submit your choices. I've actually had a name "go away" on me in fifteen minutes time so I know it can happen! Of course, you can make a minor adjustment, like a tiny spelling change, for the name you prefer and you will be good to go. The names just can't be identical. If a name for an LLC has been used and that LLC has expired, in many cases, you will be free to reuse that name. Whatever name you select the letters "LLC" must be added at the end.

Step Two

Registering the LLC. I may have slightly jumped the gun in step one but I'm hoping the repetition will help. To be perfectly clear, you must register the LLC and the LLC name at the same time, so when I mentioned locking in the name of your business, you must also have the additional required company information at your fingertips. The good news is the necessary information is very basic. All that's required to form the LLC is the (1) business name, (2) business purpose, (3) your name, (4) the physical address of the business, (5) the mailing address for the business, (6) your signature and the date and, finally, (7) pay the fee. This is very basic contact information so there should not be any objections to giving this to the appropriate agency. They simply want to know who is in charge and how to get in touch with them when needed.

As far as filing is concerned, in most states the forms are readily available online so that's not a problem. Electronic filing is also an option in many states and, in reality, is the quickest and most efficient method of forming an LLC. I use electronic or "e-file" exclusively when filing for an LLC. I have filed for several LLC's while outside the United States so the convenience and versatility of e-file is hard to match as compared to conventional channels.

It's important to note it is not necessary to "qualify" in order to form an LLC. To my knowledge, if you apply for an LLC and pay the appropriate fee you will get your LLC. There is no approval and/or acceptance process so if your information is accurate you will receive your certificate by USPS mail within a week or instantly via email if you e-file. So, at this point you will be legal.

Step Three

In step two, I went through a detailed explanation of how to form a legal LLC. It is very important to note the procedure in step two applied to an LLC which involved only one person. If two or more people are going to be involved in the LLC you must create what is known as an *Operating Statement*. The operating statement is nothing more than a contract agreement between individuals involved in the LLC. Also, there must be at least one designated managing member for every LLC who is authorized to sign documents on behalf of the other members.

As you may guess this process can be very complex when more than one person is involved. Right about now you should be saying to yourself: "I may have to retain the services of an attorney.", and you would be absolutely correct! This is a very important phase in your business career because any mistakes here and, to put it bluntly, you could very well have a huge headache for many years to come. Now is the time to do your research and locate the most knowledgeable attorney you can find who has the necessary experience to compose a nice, air-tight LLC operating statement. They will be well worth their fee.

You may be tempted to use an online legal service to save money but this is a terrible idea. These services are fine for some of your legal needs but an LLC operating statement is most definitely ***Not*** one of them. All LLC operating statements have their own unique features so I can assure you this is definitely not a "one size fits all" situations. If you consider yourself to be an extremely lucky person and choose to go the online route then more power to you but you better hope your luck doesn't run out!

A good operating statement can easily be ten to twelve pages long but this is a very rough estimate. The number of pages in an operating statement does not dictate how good or bad it is but there are some guidelines. I will say unless the print is quite small if you get an operating statement that's much less than six or eight pages then, you may not have much protection. If the statement is extremely long then you may be getting charged for a lot of fluff. As I mentioned earlier, do your homework and get a reputable attorney.

A really good operating statement will give details on how the LLC members should behave in the process of doing business. More importantly, it will give details of what to do when things start going wrong. This is what is known as an *"exit strategy"*. When everything is going fine, all is well with the members. But, when issues arise, remedies must be in place before they occur. You see, when everything is going fine everyone will agree on most issues, but when things start going wrong then, most likely, no one is going to agree on anything! This is why it is so extremely important to agree on things that can go wrong while everything is going fine. You and the other members will have money invested in the business and no one wants to lose their investment so your operating statement must be air tight with all "t's crossed and i's dotted". Once again, I am being brief with this information since professional legal advice from a reputable, qualified attorney will yield much better results for you and your business.

Forming a Corporation

We just completed a brief discussion for forming an LLC which gives protection for your personal assets as does a corporation. For the record, there are many features of LLCs and corporations that are very similar. However, corporations are much more complex and structured than an LLC. To complicate matters more, there are many different types of corporations so forming a corporation is not the best strategy for a startup business. That said, once your business expands to a certain point you will most certainly want to consider this structure.

A good accountant is very important for any successful business to thrive and grow. When the decision is made to form a corporation an accountant, and specifically a *certified public accountant,* is an absolute necessity. There are several types of corporations and, from a tax standpoint, these types of corporations can give you some very noticeable tax benefits. When you start rolling in the big bucks the corporation structure will be your best bet but your accountant should be the person to make that decision.

Unlike an LLC, a corporation can be very expensive to form and maintain. The legal and accounting services alone can be a fairly substantial expense but, remember, you will be making some really good money at this time, so the expense shouldn't be a major concern. As you know, these are business expenses which are tax deductible. Since you are a shrewd business person you do; however, want to continue watching these additional costs.

One of the greatest pitfalls of business is to be careless with expenditures once larger sums of money are being made. Now that your business has become very successful and is enjoying substantial earnings, this is when the services of your accountant are most needed. Since your accountant is your primary financial advisor, he or she should help you keep an eye on your income and expenses and, also, alert you when it would be a good idea to form a corporation.

In order for a corporation to be a corporation it must behave like a corporation. In order to behave like a corporation there are a number of things that must be done. A corporation generally requires much more effort in the form of paperwork and time so this must be factored in as an indirect expense. The State Corporation Commission or your appropriate agency has fairly strict guidelines on forms that must be filed and when they should be filed. The IRS and the federal government also have requirements so you really have to be on your toes to stay on top of all the paperwork. In both cases there are stiff fines and penalties for not following the appropriate guidelines so pay close attention because this could be a make or break situation for you and your corporation.

Now that I have scared you half to death, let me assure you that you will still want to consider a corporation business structure when your company reaches a certain size. The ongoing paperwork can get a little tedious and nerve wracking but the benefits are well worth the effort. As the owner of the business, you may not be doing this paperwork anyway. In my case I delegated this process to one of my highly qualified office staff members and my contribution was to confirm the appropriate paperwork was filed properly and in a timely manner.

Okay, I think I'm going to go ahead and wrap up this section on business structures and leave the rest to the professionals. I hope this at least gives you a reasonable overview of business structures and the possibilities. Keep in mind, I am not the authority on this subject so please contact an accountant and/or attorney in your specific area for exact details and further recommendations.

SECTION 9

Advertising and Marketing

It's Show Time!

I think you will agree, this has been an exciting process. It's been a lot of work but it's worth it. If you are more excited than ever, then you should be! This is when the fun begins! It's now time to reap the benefits of all your hard work but you are not quite done yet.

Now it's time to get customers coming through your doors. To be sure, you should have actually started this process before your business opened its doors. Getting the word out early in the process serves two very constructive purposes. First, it lets potential customers know in advance they will soon be in a position to bring their vehicle to a person who they will know and trust. The best way to do this is to use the marketing concept known as "networking". Networking is the act of going to places where you find groups of people and start shaking hands and talking to them. This is the all-time best way to build rapport with your future customers and sell your service. I will discuss this process in depth later in this section.

The second and equally important reason to put the word out early has to do with goal setting. You see, if you start telling everyone you know what your plans are and you chicken out then; "You got a whole lot of 'splainin' to do!". Believe me, it's not a good feeling when people you know and come in contact with on a daily basis think you are a quitter. This is actually a great motivator if you chose to use this situation in a positive way. You see, this will be that extra bit of motivation you will need to call on to help you follow through and achieve your dreams. When friends and associates ask about progress with your business, instead of saying; "I've changed my mind, I think I'll quit.", you can hold your head high and report; "The action plan is in place and I will be opening on schedule!". Now that's impressive!

Lifeblood of Your Business

Advertising is the lifeblood of any business and that includes the automotive business. It is as essential to a business as air and water is to your body. If you want to keep your business alive you must *advertise.* Even after you have achieved your maximum work load you will still want to advertise. On the surface that doesn't make much sense but the key to advertising is training potential customers' minds so that when they think of auto repair they think of you and your auto repair facility. With effective advertising you will have customers showing up at your doorstep in numbers. Through the use of clear, concise, repetitive advertising customers will come to your auto repair facility without even considering your competition. Now, this is powerful stuff!

There are so many methods for advertising and marketing it would require another book to do the subject justice. In this section I will give you all of the necessary information you will need to develop an effective advertising and marketing plan. This advertising program will not be inexpensive but, on the other hand, it will not cost anywhere close to what you may think. There are many ways to get lots of "bang for your buck" and I will be more than happy to give you all of the necessary details. Creative advertising is so exciting because, with little or no expense, you will have customers flooding to your door step.

As I mentioned earlier in this guide, once you get the customer in the door of your reception area you will implement my recommendations and, as a result, you will have that customer for life. As the saying goes, "the customer is King", and not to forget the ladies, "the customer is also Queen", and if you treat them as such, they will never go anywhere else. This tip alone will save you many thousands of dollars on advertising because these customers will be repeat customers. And, at the same time they will be spreading the news of your repair facility to everyone they know *and that doesn't cost you one red cent.*

Networking

As I mentioned earlier in the "It's Show Time" section of this guide, the all-time best and most effective marketing tool for your business is "networking". If you are not familiar with this term it is simply the process of going out and meeting people and selling your services. You see, when people meet you they immediately form an opinion of you. Now, that could be good or it could be bad and naturally if you are planning on going into business and develop a strong customer base, that opinion of you better be good. This is when that all important first impression really counts.

In networking, the "meet and greet" will be a similar event as the meeting you will have with your new customers when they enter your place of business for the first time. The wording will be different but the concept is exactly the same. It's as simple as: "How are you? My name is Alex. I am in the process of starting my own auto repair facility and will be open by the first of the month. I would greatly appreciate your business. Here is my business card. Feel free to call me anytime if you have any questions. Thank you for your time and have a great day! See you soon!".

Make absolutely certain you are smiling through this entire process because your smile will contribute more towards winning this new customer than anything else you can do. The real beauty of networking is that it is basically free. You will be networking when you go to the grocery store, a sporting event, a school class play, a dance, or a party at a friend's house.

You are going to be at many of these places anyway so you may as well share your business plans with all of the people you come in contact with. Trust me, they will be extremely interested. Really! So, have at it. Feel free to share all of the important details with them. Explain to them how clean and neat your shop will be and that your facility will be run "by the book" and in a very professional manner. Your office and waiting room will be clean and neat and your office staff will be courteous. They will be impressed with your enthusiasm and your attention to detail.

As a side note: you may have noticed earlier I mentioned handing out your business card during your meet and greet networking encounter. Call me old fashioned but business cards still work like a champ. They are very inexpensive and quite effective but you must make sure they are professional, legible and contain clear, concise information. Business cards give you a lot of bang for your buck so please don't ignore them when networking.

One of the best networking opportunities is to join one or more non-profit organizations. You will be exposed to lots of very good potential customers who would love to meet you. A word of caution though: if your heart is not in it then people will notice. This can, and most likely will, create a negative effect so if you are not dedicated to a particular cause then please don't get involved.

Through this whole process you have been doing a lot of talking so now it's time to socialize and let the other person talk for a while. The best method of getting people to talk about themselves is to ask them an open ended question such as where they work, where they live, if they have kids, or what their hobbies are. You know, normal social conversation. Don't talk about automobiles unless they choose to.

This is your opportunity to bond with this individual on a personal level and show them you care about them as a person. It is very important you are sincere with these actions. If you show this individual you care about them as a person they will feel comfortable you will certainly care about their automobile. You have now acquired a lifelong customer who will also recommend you to others and the best part is it happened at no cost whatsoever to you! I think you would agree, it doesn't get much better than this.

About now there are a fair number of people reading this guide who are thinking; "This is all good and fine but I'm not comfortable walking up to people and starting a conversation". To that I say: "Welcome to the club!". I was that way many years ago but I learned to overcome this situation primarily out of necessity. I wanted to develop a larger customer base and I knew networking was the secret to achieving this goal and in the most cost effective manner. I realized if other people could start conversations with new people then I knew I could to. So, I just went out and did it!

Once I learned the amazing benefits of networking I knew I had to at least give it a try. After all, there was all that extra customer traffic out there available at little to no cost! There was no way I was going to ignore this opportunity so I decided to do some research on the topic.

Come to find out the vast majority of people are thrilled when someone comes up and wants to talk to them. It actually makes them feel special because they rationalize they must appear to be friendly and approachable if a perfect stranger can walk up and start talking to them. What a relief: all this time I thought I was imposing on people when I approached them and started talking. All the while I was actually making their day. That concept really created a monster because at that point I started talking to anyone who got within twenty-five feet of me. As I think about it, an extremely high percentage of people I came in contact with quite often became loyal customers. That could explain why our shop was busy day in and day out, week after week, month after month and year after year for as long as I can remember. It worked for me and I know it will work for you.

TV Commercials

TV advertising can be rather expensive but it can also be extremely productive. Unfortunately, if you live in an extremely large city or metropolitan area, TV ads could be out of the question. With that said, I would check anyway because even the largest TV stations are willing to work some really great package deals so at least give them a chance to make a presentation. To my knowledge most if not all TV stations will set up an account so you can make payments that will fit your budget. Make sure this expense is figured in so you have funds available when the bill comes in. TV ads can seem to be a bit pricey but they can be quite beneficial in the promotion of your business. Although my shop was constantly busy, I rarely if ever missed a month doing TV ads. Allow me to explain why I'm so persistent with this subject, and no, I'm not in cahoots with the TV stations!

The reason TV advertising is so important is that it is indirectly related to networking. The point of networking is you get to meet lots of people and have them like you while, at the same time, you will be trying to make a case for why they should bring their vehicle to you for repairs. I think you would agree with me, you could network "till the cows come home" and you would not be able to come in contact with everyone in your service area. What if there was a way to get lots of people to see you and get the opportunity to like you, and at the same time, convince them to bring their vehicle to your facility for repairs? If you think this sounds like I am talking about television advertising you would be exactly right.

About now, you may be taking a deep breath because you are thinking that: if this is my potential customer's opportunity to see me, listen to me and to like me, then I must be in the TV commercial. And, you would be absolutely correct with this assumption. Maybe you think you could never be in a TV commercial but you are going to find that when you are in business you are going to be able to do a lot of things you never thought you could do and this is one of them. Like I said before, this is show time and now it's for real! This is not a dress rehearsal!! You didn't come this far just to fall on your face so it's time to dig your heels in and go for it. Remember, you are confident you will have the absolute best auto repair facility with the best shop team and office staff in your area. All you have to do now is take this confidence combined with a big smile and let the whole world know that you are the best of the best and if they will just give you the opportunity you will prove it to them.

Now, for a nice little (actually big) twist to this concept. This is like bonus points for your television advertising dollar. Bear with me for a moment while I set the stage. If you have been following my advice to this point there should be a lady or ladies running the office and reception area and the guys should be responsible for shop operations. Now, to be sure, the opposite arrangement could also be true. I'm just saying that, based on my experience, ladies are most productive in the office and the guys tend to excel in the shop area. Once again, my primary objective is staying out of trouble with the ladies. The guys fully understand where I'm coming from on this issue.

Anyway, the point I'm trying to make (in somewhat of a roundabout way) is there should be at least one lady and at least one guy working as a team in the operation of an auto repair business. Here's the deal: *both of you will be starring in your TV commercial!* This next comment is very important: *you may or may not be a couple but when the camera is rolling you must act like a very happy "All American" couple* if you expect to extract the maximum benefit from your TV advertising dollar. As you are saying your lines it is important that you smile and look at each other briefly, making eye contact and then back at the camera. *It is important to realize that what you say in the commercial won't matter nearly as much as your appearance and your body language.*

The most important aspect of this approach is the viewer and potential customer must look at this commercial and think to themselves: "What a happy, attractive, honest couple. I would really like to see them make it. I'm going to take my car to their shop because I'm sure they will do a great job. I would really love to meet them in person!". Remember, our focus is to market to the ladies so this is the image you will want to project in order to attract this special group of customers.

As with your business name, if you want to get the maximum benefit from your advertising dollar it is important you sell emotion first and facts second. The viewer will soon forget the facts but that "feel good" image will stay with them forever. Remember, selling emotion in any form of advertising is the single most productive technique to get the greatest return on your advertising dollar.

But wait, there's more! You can take this concept and bump it up a notch. If either, or both of you have kids then get them in the commercial too. Don't forget about your pet or your office mascot. They can also be in the commercial. People love seeing kids and pets in commercials. All of these little tricks add substantially to the effectiveness of your TV ads. People will actually stop by your shop just to visit your cute pet and will most likely make an appointment for their car before they leave. This happened to me on quite a few occasions so I know it works.

While I'm on the subject of pets here is an example of how to implement one of my networking suggestions. This is only for those individuals who are sincere and dedicated to helping homeless pets. I would highly recommend dedicating at least a portion of your TV ads to help promote pet shelters and spay/neuter clinics. About now you are thinking to yourself: "What? I'm running an automotive shop, not a pet center!", and you would be correct. Here's the deal: there are a lot of pet lovers out there and they love people who love pets. Keep in mind, these people also drive cars so now you see the critical connection. If these people love you and love your cause they cannot help but show up at your doorstep and want you to repair their automobile.

Now it's time to put your words into action. This is when your indirect networking becomes direct networking. You see, your TV advertising (indirect networking) now gives you a foot in the door for the many pet shelters and now you can do your direct networking. As I mentioned earlier, networking while performing community service is the most effective networking you can do. Just remember, your heart has to be in it to be effective so sincerity is the key.

Let's take it a step further. Since many pet shelters are non-profit organizations all monetary donations are tax deductible. This is a quite legitimate donation that would never be questioned by the IRS. Make sure you have a signed receipt and you are good to go. At this point you have placed your "money where your mouth is" so now you have truly proved your dedication to the cause. And, now you can include in your advertising, as well as promotional cards and brochures; "A portion of your profits go to charity". Believe me when I say, your customer base will increase dramatically. Of course, this technique applies to *All* charities. Please do not ignore this valuable information.

Sorry that I appeared to get a little off track with this subject but I promised you all of the minute details and this is simply another important little detail that can make a big difference for your business. I promised I would not waste your time with insignificant information so please accept and implement these important concepts. Your success depends on it.

As a side note: another technique that works quite well is to inject *Humor* into your commercials. This applies primarily to TV and radio ads but you can use it anywhere. Once again, you will be selling *Emotion*. Laughter associated with humor is one of the most positive emotions a person can experience. This takes the feel good factor and bumps it up a notch. Anything that makes people laugh has to be good. There is a theory that states: "It's not that people laugh because they are happy, but instead, they are happy because they laugh". So, if you can make your potential customers laugh, which will in turn make them feel happy, there will be an improved chance they will remember you. Being remembered is one of our primary goals with advertising. Anything you can do to condition your customer's mind and cause them to automatically contact you whenever they need an auto repair is your ultimate objective.

With all this said, make absolutely certain it is good clean family humor. Do not use any innuendos that may be suggestive in any way. Even though the kids won't get it, you still don't want to try anything off color. Remember, we are trying to present the All American, Clean Cut image so any questionable content could be a real turnoff.

Something I have noticed in some ads which I also feel is a turn off is when one person in the commercial pokes fun at the other to indicate superior intelligence. Personally I am never impressed with this technique. It is much better to make positive, light hearted comments to each other. The viewer response will be noticeably improved. Keep in mind, the two individuals in the commercial will most likely be a lady and a guy so, in the interest of maintaining that All American, Clean Cut, couples' image I would keep everything as amiable as possible. The way I see it too many couples argue, bicker and make too many snide remarks to each other so we do not want to participate in this behavior.

You could make what may seem to be a harmless comment but it could affect a potential customer negatively. We never want this to happen. Keep in mind, this could be a potential customer who needs a profitable engine replacement and you just lost the opportunity to get the job. Once again, this little detail could get you that one extra job you were really hoping for so be nice and be positive when including humor in your commercials. Remember, we want to keep that "feel good" emotion alive and well!

Open House

Even though your shop may be open Monday through Friday, plan your grand opening on a Saturday. Hold an open house so potential customers can tour the shop area on a day when they have plenty of time with not much else to do. This will give you and your shop staff plenty of time to discuss any issues a potential customer may have concerning an auto repair.

In addition, have a free diagnostic clinic as part of your open house. That will definitely keep you busy. This is a fairly expensive service so offering a free engine scan will get your potential customer's attention. You are almost certain to get a few really good jobs from this service. The appearance of a lot of vehicles in and around the shop will make you look busy. Customers like this because people tend to frequent establishments if they think others do too. You can also use my trick of having all of your friends show up with their cars. That will make you look extra super busy and that's even better.

Once again, I should mention your insurance must cover visits by customers and, if so, this event should qualify. Your shop area is going to be neat as a pin so hopefully that should prevent an accident. Make sure the floor is extra clean and dry to prevent any slip hazards.

The Internet

Internet advertising is one of the most powerful advertising tools available to boost your workload. The instant a potential customer searches for "auto repair" it is essential for your company website to show up at the top of the list. There are several tricks of the trade to accomplish this objective but paying a fee will guarantee you will be front and center. Your professional website designer should handle this detail for you. A "first page" search position has a strong psychological effect in that, potential customers will assume you are the best since you are at the top of the list. This assumption will be correct because you will be the best!

The fee to be placed in the top position can vary depending on the size of your market area. The good news is you can use this feature until you get solidly established and then you can terminate if you like. I think you will find this is very cost effective advertising since it will deliver an incredible response. The only way you would be able to justify canceling this service is if you are so covered up with work you couldn't take in any more jobs.

Another way to get "first page" positioning is to use search engine optimization and algorithms to your benefit. For sure, algorithms can be a bit of an "elusive beast" since the guidelines change on a fairly regular basis. Generally speaking, your positioning will depend on your website content. The most important aspect to remember with regards to website content is to always keep it updated and make sure all content contains meaningful and useful information. Rest assured this subject is far more complex than that but this should give you a brief notion as to some of the possibilities. Tutorials are available that will help with using search engine optimization and algorithms so, for more information, check out some of these sites.

I would highly recommend a nice, professionally designed website. Make sure you have lots of good pictures. Be sure you include the shop, the office and all of the staff members. Make certain you also include pictures of one your most important staff members: your office mascot. Remember, your mascot has top billing so feature him or her on your home page. Your mascot doesn't have to be in all of the pictures but the more the better.

Make absolutely certain you have really good, clear, concise directions to your shop so potential customers can easily make it to your front door. Of course, make sure you include all of your contact information. I would also include a feature that allows customers to schedule their own appointments and an auto responder with a personal sounding message so your customer will be assured you are "On It". Your office staff can then email the customer with a confirmation.

Depending on the customer, this could be a great opportunity to make a phone call and give confirmation. If you think they are not too busy, a friendly phone call will work wonders toward really great customer relations.

I would recommend you periodically check your own website to confirm all of the features are working properly. You could have customers and potential customers trying to make appointments and if your web site is not working properly they may not be receiving a response. As you may guess this would not be good. An easy to navigate website that functions properly is an absolute necessity if your automotive business is to succeed.

Social Media

I will be the first to admit, I know very little about social media but I am definitely learning everything I can and as fast as I can. For sure, this is one of the most powerful sources of free or minimal cost advertising you can find anywhere. I am not certain as to why it's called social media and not "Digital Networking" because that's what it actually is: networking. It just happens to be the "virtual version" of going out and meeting people face to face so it's still networking.

If you recall, networking is the process of going out and meeting people in person so they can get to know you, then they can "Like You" and, as a result, will become lifelong customers. Now you can see where social media acquired its roots. The concept is very basic but has the capability of producing incredible results. Keep in mind, face-to-face networking should never be replaced by social media networking. Feel free to call me "Old Fashioned" but I still believe direct, face-to-face networking will yield the best, most reliable and loyal customer base but its' reach and scope is somewhat limited. Remember, earlier in this section I highly recommended television advertising as a method of expanding this networking reach and scope but even television has its limitations.

So, in comes Social Media: otherwise known as "Networking on Steroids!!". To my knowledge I am not aware of any other method of reaching a maximum number of potential customers in a way that will allow you to come in contact with them, get them to like you and, then, convert them into lifelong customers. Since social media is so widely used it is one of the most reliable and accepted methods of getting in contact with individuals and potential customers. Granted, people are not meeting you in person but you are still, with the use of proper techniques and proven methods, in a position of presenting yourself as a credible and honest person who potential customers would prefer to do business with.

Of all the volumes of information related to gaining maximum results from social media the most important is to present yourself as honest and credible. You must understand and take to heart social media can also have an opposite and negative effect on your efforts to build your business.

As a little refresher course on this subject: you may recall in the section devoted to "The Customer", and specifically in the segment dedicated to ladies being your "Best Customers", I commented as to the importance of keeping them happy. I also commented on the fact they will appreciate everything you do and will send lots of referral work your way.

Now, this is primarily for the guys but the lady repair shop owners must listen up as well. If you happen to use poor judgement and attempt to do something dishonest and/or unethical with one or more of your lady customers this is when social media will come back to "bite" you. In other words: "The Ladies Will Do You IN!!". And, I mean Big Time!

We all know the ladies love to socialize and communicate so it's easy to see why social media is an area with a high female participation. Now, you may say: "I don't like social media and I'm not going to use it so social media will have no effect on me". Well, I think you can see that, based on the previous information, social media can and will have a huge effect on you and your business. It could cost you your business! The point I want to make is this: whether you participate in social media or not your customers are free to make comments about you as they see fit and there is very little you can do about it!

So, the take away from this little "refresher" course is this: you must be honest and take care of all your customers; especially your lady customers and your business will thrive. But, if you are dishonest and don't take care of your customers, both ladies and guys, your business will perish! To be sure, this event will all be thanks to social media!

As I mentioned earlier in this segment on social media, I commented that my knowledge with regard to Social media was somewhat limited but I was hot on the trail for acquiring this knowledge. Thanks to my very good friend Soraya who downloaded an excellent social media audio book on my IPod, I have gained substantial knowledge with regard to the social media arena. Since there are a multitude of great publications on the market dedicated to social media, I will spare you the minute details in this publication. I do; however, have and important overall "take away" from what I have learned about social media.

First and foremost: never attempt to sell your service on social media. The only thing you want to sell on social media is *Yourself*!! And, when I say "sell" this should be a very subtle "soft sell". The point of social media is to get people to "*Like You*" and, then, offer a few subtle hints along the way that will arouse their curiosity as to the details of exactly what you do. So, you should, in a very indirect and subtle way, let your followers know you are in the auto repair business. You must be careful because many social media sites will "bump you off" of their site if they think you are promoting a business. Social media was originally intended for "social encounters" but has now evolved into something more, but you still must be very cautious as to your content.

The very best approach is to simply offer a few automotive tips on your social media site(s). Then, simply wait for your followers to ask you how you know so much about auto repair and this is when you let them know you are in the auto repair business. You see, what social media will do is create curiosity in a potential customer which will, in turn, entice them to pursue your service. The key here is this: never allow the customer to think you are pursuing them but rather, have them think they are pursuing you and your service. They will be so proud of themselves for making such a wonderful find: Your Auto Repair Facility!! And, it's as simple as that!

As promised, I will not take a lot of your time explaining social media; there are many experts in this field so I will gladly delegate this task to these individuals. I admit I am a bit behind the curve with regard to social media as compared to the younger generation but you better keep an eye over shoulder because, very soon, I will be right behind you. My best advice with regard to social media is: "Go For It and Do It" and your auto repair business will THRIVE!!

Newspaper Ads

When I bring up newspaper advertising I guess you think I've gone from one extreme to the other and actually you are right. Believe it or not there are a fair number of people who still don't use computers. These are smart, well-educated people who, for whatever reason, stick to the original method of delivering information. They believe, "If it ain't broke don't fix it". You never can tell, they could be right and all of us computer people could be the ones headed down the wrong path. Whatever the case may be, they still need a place to take their car to have it repaired so, if you have the good sense to run newspaper ads you can include this very important group of customers in our work load. After all, keeping the shop full is one of our primary objectives.

Nowadays newspaper companies are struggling to stay afloat so they have a tendency to offer some really great deals on advertising. I would say if you are going to run a newspaper ad make it large enough that it will be hard to miss. It will cost more to do a large ad but a small ad that blends in and is not seen is of no value at all and that would be a total waste of money.

My strategy as far as newspaper ads were concerned was to run a menu of services with basic prices. It is always good to give prices for your services so your potential customer has some idea as to what a particular repair may cost. Make sure you state exactly what will be included in each service. Also, make sure it's quite clear in the ad this is the basic service and any other parts and labor will be additional. Do this all in legible print so your potential customer doesn't feel as though they are being misled. If they suspect this you will have lost them before you ever got them. One of the worst things you can do is make a repair to a customer's car and then have to explain these details after the fact.

Keep in mind when running newspaper ads printed material has a tendency to be permanent so make absolutely certain you proofread the ad before it goes to print. And, get a copy of the proofed ad to keep on file. Newspapers have been known to make mistakes from time to time so it is extremely important you proofread the actual ad as it will appear in the paper. If there are any mistakes you must contact them immediately to make the correction and disclose in writing or email they made a mistake. Once the corrections have been made and you have given final approval, your ad goes to print. You have done your job so everything should be fine. But, you may find, upon inspection of the ad, there is an error. As you may guess, this is not good! The preventative measures didn't work so now you will have to move to corrective measures.

Sad to say, but you will now have to honor what was in print even though it was not your mistake. At this point I would have a little "heart to heart" discussion with the general manager of the newspaper concerning this dilemma and demand that you be compensated for the inconvenience. Quite often they will reduce the cost of the ad but sometimes that's not quite enough. At this point you have two options. One solution is to refuse to pay and go to court over the issue. I would consider this to be somewhat excessive and definitely counterproductive.

This is what I would do in this situation and you could also apply this to other similar situations as well. The first thing I would do is make an appointment with the newspaper general manager. This should be a face to face meeting so you can explain in person how dissatisfied you are with their service and, that you plan to curtail or eliminate their services from your advertising budget. In other words: "Fix it or you're fired!!". At this point you have done everything you can do so now it's time to leave and get back to work. Simply state your case and leave: the ball is now in their court. You cannot waste any more of your valuable time with this issue!

Now, it's time to take lemons and make lemonade. The first thing you will do is pull out your proofed copy of the ad and then cut the actual ad out of the paper. Next, fasten these two ads to a backing in such a fashion they can be displayed in a location visible to all customers entering your reception area. In addition, add a caption that states something like this:

"Here is the proofed copy of our newspaper ad and this is the actual ad. Please notice our proofed copy stated our basic brake service is $89.95 but the actual ad stated our basic brake service is $69.95. This issue is currently not resolved. This is clearly an error on the part of the newspaper but, as a service to our customers, we will honor this offer for the duration of the promotion. We appreciate your business and thank you".

This process will give you added credibility which translates into increased customer loyalty and this is always good for business. Once again you took a bad situation and by using sound business practices, ended with a positive result. Behaving in a mature manner, remaining level headed and being decisive will always generate a happy ending.

Well, it looks like I got off on one of my infamous tangents again but I felt this was a necessary detour since this was a stressful experience I had in the process of running my auto repair facility. I strictly apologize to all of the wonderful news print operations out there; you are doing a great job and I expect the best for you in the future. By the way, my issue was finally resolved to my complete satisfaction and everyone "lived happily ever after". The newspaper admitted it was their error and since I was a good longtime customer they refunded the ad fee plus an additional credit for my next ad. I continued using newspaper advertising but from then on they were extra, extra careful to get my ads correct. I really appreciated their efforts on my behalf.

As I mentioned before, this scenario applies to any similar situation. Remember to document everything and then be very much up front when something like this happens. A situation like this could damage your credibility and we never want that to happen. Although this lesson was somewhat at my expense, I promised you I would share my personal experiences so you would not have to learn this stuff the hard way. I felt this was a great example.

In the final analysis, newspaper advertising can and will be quite beneficial in developing a solid customer base. Keep in mind, these are customers who you would most likely not reach using any other method so it is well worth the expense. So, it's a definite "Old Fashioned" *Yes* to newspaper advertising!

Radio Advertising

I have very mixed emotions about radio advertising. I used radio advertising mainly because several of my really good customers were either DJ's or worked at various radio stations. The rates for radio advertising were much better than TV advertising but I felt as though I was getting only half of the benefit. You see, I could speak to my potential customers by means of a radio broadcast but they could not see me and therefore were unable to form a full opinion of me. As a result, the visual aspect of the ad was lost. Based on what they heard, they were fairly sure they liked me but it would have been nice if they could have seen me to make their final decision.

The other thing to consider is the fact listeners are, most likely, working or doing their favorite hobby and have the radio on for the music and are really not paying very close attention to the ads. This is why it is so very important you place your ads in the right time slot and with the correct demographic (group). Basically, a demographic is a group of individuals with similar likes, habits and tastes. There is plenty of data as to what, when, where and how each of these demographics (groups) spent their dollars. This information is readily available on the internet but, to anyone who is in advertising, this information is second nature.

I could go on for days discussing this subject but I'm sure you get the message. It all boils down to the fact you want to focus on reaching the maximum number of individuals who are most in need of your services. It is very important you not use your favorite radio station unless it pinpoints that specific demographic you are looking for. Remember, you are in business now so every dollar counts toward your bottom line. At least for now, personal preference must take a back seat to making money so make sure you go with the station that will generate the maximum benefit for your advertising dollar.

Once you have selected the station that will reach the customer base you want to focus on, now it's time to decide on the right time slots. Through my experience the very best time slots are during morning and evening drive times with the evening drive time being the best. Evening drive time is the best because your potential customer, although a little tired, will be more relaxed and receptive to what you have to say. There are several really good reasons that drive time, whether morning or evening, works the best.

First, it goes without saying (but I will say it anyway), most working people will be in their cars going back and forth to work during drive time hours. Let's say they are driving down the road and their car skips or misses or makes a funny sound and then about five minutes later your ad comes on the radio. You know what they say, "timing is everything". I'm willing to bet as soon as they have the opportunity you will be getting a call from this potential customer and, hopefully, they will be making an appointment for you to repair their vehicle.

Second: there will be at least one, if not more, additional people in the car going to or from work. With the advent of carpooling there could be as many as four or five people in a single car. Now I think you can see the potential for doing radio ads in this time slot. For thirty minutes to an hour you have a totally captive audience. Granted, most of the people in the car are passengers but I bet all of them have cars at home and, as it happens, they all will require repairs sooner or later. This is when a nice, clear, concise radio commercial would definitely hit the spot. Even better, is to run multiple commercials back to back but try to not run them too close together. If you run them too close together it gets to be a bit irritating and we don't want that to happen.

A nice pleasant ad with you talking will help potential customers better receive your message even if it is of a repetitive nature. Although some of the passengers will be sleeping, the repetitive nature of the ad will enter their subconscious mind and they will still get the message. As a side note, there are studies that show even if the volume is turned down to where they can barely hear it, the subconscious mind can still process the information and place it in a potential customer's memory bank. Now that's some really good stuff.

Remember, radio advertising should be clear and concise with you (the owner) speaking to your potential customer about the benefits of you repairing their vehicle. Include the emotional effect by mentioning something like: "Your family's safety is very important to us and, with a well-maintained vehicle, your travels will be safer and more fun.", and with this comment, you will really grab their attention.

Once again, make absolutely certain you use drive time slots and specifically evening drive time. It may cost a bit more but it is well worth the additional expense. This is when your potential customers are in their car and in a captive position whereby they can do little else but listen to the radio. In addition, there will most likely be more people in the car due to the "Car Pool" affect so, you will be getting that extra benefit of reaching more people with your advertising dollar.

My best advice: always listen to what the station sales representative recommends because they will be most up to date on current market conditions. Since different market areas perform differently, pay close attention to what your radio sales rep has to say. They will work hard to make certain you get the best results because they want you to keep advertising with them.

In the end, there are many, many methods of reaching out and acquiring potential customers but these were the ones that worked best for me. Remember to never let your guard down and stop advertising. Your name and your business name must be permanently embedded in your customers', or potential customers' minds so make certain they think only of you when it's time to have their vehicle repaired. Quite often this requires a persistent and continuous advertising effort because you don't want any of the customers you worked so hard for to have a weak moment and stray on you. Never forget: there is a lot of competition out there so do not get complacent when it comes to marketing and advertising. If you let your guard down someone else will come along and "run right over you". We will never allow this to happen! Advertise, Advertise, Advertise!!

SECTION 10

Business Affilliations

Automotive Aftermarket Association

My very best advice is to join your local auto aftermarket association as soon as possible! For individuals who have been in the auto repair business for many years, you may be more familiar with the term "garage owners association". Whichever term you prefer, join as soon as you have made your mind up to open your auto repair facility. Once you join, *you and your membership must remain active for as long as you are in the automotive business.* This could be the single most important decision you will make with your automotive repair business so please don't make the fatal mistake and ignore this advice. The concept of "power in numbers" could never be truer than for a small business owner. When a group of people unite for a common cause there is no telling what can be accomplished. If not for the automotive aftermarket associations and the auto parts associations there would be few, if any, independent auto repair facilities remaining in existence.

The reason independent shops would disappear is, among other things, the new car manufacturers would never voluntarily give up technical data to them. Without this data it would be all but impossible to repair many of the automobiles on the road today. The new car manufacturers invested a fair amount of money in this technology and data so this strategy is perfectly understandable. Under the same circumstances I would be tempted to do the same thing. You see, the motivation for the new car manufacturers is the same as ours: Profit. Not only is their motivation to make a profit, it is to also maximize those profits. So, giving up their technology and data to independent repair shops would negatively affect their bottom line. The point I would like to make is this: the new car manufacturers are business people just like we are and they have to look out for their best interests just like we do. So, voluntarily giving up their data would be out of the question. This scenario would basically put independent auto repair facilities and aftermarket suppliers out of business.

In comes the auto aftermarket association and the aftermarket auto parts associations to put the world on notice *this isn't going to happen.* This is when the power in numbers concept comes into play. When you have a whole lot of little voices uniting into one giant voice you will be noticed. The message in this case was: "We need this technical data to survive and be competitive in the auto repair industry!!". It worked because the important data required to repair the newer automobiles is now available to independent repair shops throughout the country.

About now you may be starting to feel bad for the new car manufacturers because they are getting a raw deal but actually it was the customer who was going to get the raw deal. You see, if a person had a late model vehicle and wanted to have it repaired, and data was not available to the independent repair shops then, the dealership would be the only option. This is a huge problem because competition was removed from the equation and that will never work. In the interest of maximizing profit the dealerships could easily charge prices way above market rates and the customer would not have any other choice but to pay these inflated rates.

Of course, the government would have noticed this situation and most assuredly taken action. After all, we do have laws that address issues like this. People in government will readily admit the wheels turn slowly because there is so much activity with creating new laws and enforcing old laws there are just not enough hours in the day to address all of the issues. I'm sure everyone is familiar with the term: "The squeaky wheel gets the grease". Well, your automotive aftermarket association is your "squeaky wheel". They are there front and center letting all those concerned know we mean business and we are not going to let up until the issues are resolved. Keep in mind, we don't want it all, we are simply fighting for our fair share!

There were many, many times prior to becoming an association member when I felt quite helpless when major problems arose. My concerns would continue to fall on deaf ears because these larger business entities would not take me seriously. After all, what could one person do? Well, one person can join an association and that one person is now a whole group of people. That "helpless" feeling is now a feeling of "confidence" so, instead of getting bewildered, you are now empowered. Just the fact you can make a phone call or send an email to someone experienced (or a group of individuals) in the automotive repair business is priceless. What a relief to be in a position to get in contact with an experienced person who can either give you the answer to your issue, or can give you a list of possible solutions. This is easily worth its weight in gold.

In addition to addressing the larger business related issues you may encounter, your association members are always ready, willing and able to help with your day to day technical questions. Believe it or not, they will be more than happy to help with the diagnosis of a problem car. You would think an association member would rather have you send the vehicle to them for the diagnosis and repair but they tend to stay very busy and are unable to add to their workload.

If you know a member has knowledge and experience with a particular type of vehicle or problem simply give them a call. If you have been a diligent member and attended the meetings you will know through conversation who specializes in what area and deciding which member to call will be quite easy. As I just mentioned, they will most likely be very busy like you are so a quick call to put the bug in their ear is all you will have to do. Before you know it you will have the solution to your issue and you will be moving on to your next project.

Keep in mind, there is plenty of work for all so you will not be taking any work from them. They will most likely be covered up with work themselves. Remember, you will also be receiving calls for assistance. Even though it may not be the same person calling you, don't forget it was an association member who helped you out of a jam and now this is your opportunity to return the favor.

Now, here is a brief story of how I became involved with my automotive association. It took me almost two years to finally make up my mind to join the association in my area. I regularly received promotional information from the local association and occasionally from the national association. I was always too busy to read the information and, fairly soon after receiving the literature, it would get tossed. This went on for a good while and then, in an effort to boost membership, a few of the members started visiting shops to get people to join. After about the third visit I decided I would give them a few minutes of my time to see what they were all about. That was my lucky day. Within about an hour I was sold.

There were more than enough benefits to easily justify the membership fee so I made the decision I was IN! It's been a while now so I don't exactly recall how much the membership fee was but I can tell you that, within a week, I had a new garage owner's insurance policy that had at least twice the benefits of my old policy and cost several hundred dollars less for the year. As I said, I don't recall what my membership fee was but I can assure you it was a fraction of that amount. Believe me when I say, I took advantage of their many other benefits and saved even more.

Our association had regular meetings and when the next meeting came up I made it a point to attend. I really didn't know what to expect so I was a little nervous. After all, I was going to be in a meeting room with people who were my competition and I was sure that would be awkward. When I got to the meeting area I took a deep breath and walked into the room. Then, to my surprise no fewer than twenty people walked up to me to introduce themselves and wanted to shake my hand. What a relief! All the while, I thought these people were my competition but, instead, they were my friends and allies. What a concept! In a million years I would have never guessed that would have happened. We were all on the same team with common goals and that was really the very best benefit of all.

Here is a little added twist to the "My Story" segment in the beginning of this guide. If you recall, in that section I mentioned I did all of the planning, organizing and coordinating so everything with my automotive business would work flawlessly. You may also recall it didn't work out exactly the way I had planned. The primary issue was, in the beginning, I had no customers. I had to scramble and ask my friends to get cars in my shop so I could at least look busy. That was a very scary moment in my business life: not to mention the fact it was a lot of work.

Now that I have refreshed your memory, let me tell you how it could have been if I had joined my auto aftermarket association prior to actually opening my doors. It would have been so easy. My specialty was imported cars because that was what I had worked on for most of my life. I knew them inside and out so sticking to repairing imports made the most business sense: at least in my particular case.

When I went to the first meeting I discovered I was the only association member who specialized in import cars. None of the other guys wanted to be bothered with them and almost everyone considered them a nuisance. Honestly, imported vehicles looked more like money to me, but then, "Who am I?" laughing all the way to the bank! Well, long story short, they all absolutely, positively assured me they would send every import car that showed up at their shops directly to me. I was already busy at that time but within about two weeks, I was swamped. Now, if I had joined the association on or before opening my shop I could have been rolling from day one. If I had only known!

Your association and its members will always be there for you in your time of need. You will be in a position to access all of the experience and knowledge from individuals who have been in the automotive business for more years than they care to admit. For the record that's a long, long time. They have learned many of their lessons the hard way like I did so, they will have some really good answers for you. Your automotive aftermarket association is your "All for One, One for All" organization so everyone wins and that includes you so, once again, join your association as soon as you make the big decision to open your auto repair facility.

I promised you in the beginning that I made all of the mistakes so you would not have to, and not joining an *Automotive Aftermarket Association* is one error in judgment that should never be repeated. Fortunately, I had sense enough to finally join my association but it took a while. Promise me you will join your association as soon as you make the decision to open your automotive repair business. Please do not perpetuate my mistake.

The Better Business Bureau® and the Chamber of Commerce

Your local Better Business Bureau (BBB) and Chamber of Commerce are two great local organizations that are most definitely worthy of serious consideration when going into business. I just made the comment your Better Business Bureau and Chamber of Commerce were local organizations but they also have national connections. This should catch your attention because we are back to the concept of "Strength in Numbers". As a reminder, this is very good because, as a small business owner, our "Voice" can quite often go unnoticed but as a member of a well-recognized and accepted national organization your voice can now "Thunder" and you *Will* be noticed.

Another important detail with regards to the Better Business Bureau and Chamber of Commerce: I could have very easily incorporated these two organizations in the "Advertising and Marketing" section of this guide. You see, there are a certain number of individuals out there who view your membership in these two organizations as a determining factor as to whether they will do business with you (Or Not!). So, now you see, based on this information, you can advertise using normal channels for ever and ever and you will *Never* acquire these individuals as customers. Granted, these people are somewhat in the minority but, as you may guess, this number can add up and contribute substantially to your customer base. And, maximizing a good, high quality customer base is one of the best methods I am aware of for boosting revenue and improving "Bottom Line" results.

I am certain most who are reading this guide are familiar with these two wonderful organization so I will try to be brief. Keep in mind, these two organizations have two totally different "Mission Statements" but do share a common goal: to assist small business in their pursuit of success.

The Better Business Bureau: The primary function of the Better Business Bureau is to receive and process information related to problems or issues with businesses both large and small. To be sure, the Better Business Bureau does not have any authority, legal or otherwise, over these business. The exception would be, if you are a member and you behave in a manner contradictory to their guidelines, you could be dropped. I know the Better Business Bureau does investigate complaints to confirm accuracy but that's as far as it goes.

What the Better Business Bureau does is to compile information on business related complaints and then enter them in a data base. Generally speaking, this information is available on a national basis so it's a little difficult for a business or business owner participating in questionable business practices to "run and hide".

The really great news: if you show up in their data base as having "No Complaints" you are in good standing with the Better Business Bureau. Now, when one of your potential customers checks you out and finds you have a "clean bill of health" with the Better Business Bureau you just acquired a new life long customer!

One way to bypass this phase of the process is to simply become a member. If you are displaying credentials that verify you are a current member of the Better Business Bureau quite often a potential customer will take this as confirmation as to your status and proceed directly to becoming a full-fledged customer right on the spot! I guess the point I want stress is this: becoming a Better Business Bureau member could greatly expedite the acquisition of this customer so you will be given the opportunity to repair their vehicle and, then, generate more revenue more quickly. After all, I am sure this was one of your primary goals when you made the decision to enter the auto repair business!!

The Chamber of Commerce: As the name clearly indicates, the Chamber of Commerce was created to improve commerce or, more simply stated: assist businesses in generating more revenue from their goods and services. Although the Chamber of Commerce is a national organization, their primary impact is at the local level. I guess the best way to describe the Chamber of Commerce is they are the "Good Will Ambassadors" for business in any given area. The bottom line is this: the Chamber of Commerce wants business owners and customers to be happy so businesses will continue to operate and customers will continue to buy. It's as simple as that!!

They accomplish this task in several ways. One of the main functions of the Chamber is it acts as an intermediary or negotiator when issues that affect business owners arise. This could be the result of problems generated from a multitude of sources.

As an example: in the area where I reside they are planning a quite large road improvement project that happens to be directly in front of one of our primary shopping mall areas. Because traffic will have to be diverted and access will be limited, and for an extended period of time, this will be a very big problem for all of the merchants in this location. The extended monetary losses have been calculated in the millions of dollars and some business may be forced to close due to reduced revenues.

Now granted, these businesses have their merchants associations but their powers are somewhat limited under these conditions. This is where the Chamber of Commerce, with its local roots and national status could have a little more clout. In this case, they have managed to get this project placed on hold until our department of transportation can come up with some good, viable solutions which will resolve this issue.

Now, in the interest of efficiency I will limit my examples to this one, but, keep in mind, this is a BIG one! In my opinion, if they can ward off a large government agency then everything else should be a "cake walk".

Another service the Chamber offers is to coordinate business owners and facilitate group marketing and community efforts. Keep in mind, community efforts are the most beneficial to you, the business owner, because they are very closely tied to the concept of networking. As you may recall, in the section on "Advertising and Marketing", networking was the most effective method of convincing an individual they should become a customer at your place of business. If you made the wise decision to become a Chamber member you now have that extra bit of *credibility* and *selling yourself* to a potential customer just got a lot easier. In this case, it's all about *credibility*.

Another function the Chamber excels at is letting new residents know what kinds of businesses and services are available in a particular area. Of course, anyone can go on the internet and see what businesses in the area have to offer but there is nothing like seeing a familiar name like the Chamber of Commerce to help with purchase decisions when moving to a new area. At this point, "Trust" has been added to "Credibility" and now you will be adding to your customer base at an unbelievable rate.

In the final analysis, my best advice to any business owner, automotive or other, is to become an active member of your local Better Business Bureau and Chamber of Commerce. Of course, you will have to pay membership fees but these fees will be returned to you many times over as the result of the increase in your customer base. Although these organizations provide many valuable services the most valuable is that, by being a member, your customers and potential customers will see you as a very *Trustworthy* and *Credible* business person. And, you will be!

The beauty of this arrangement is you will be in a position to spend less time selling the benefits to a potential customer for getting their vehicle repaired at your facility. This will allow for more time to make the actual repairs which will be putting money in your pocket. There we go *Again*, making more money!!

I hope I have finally sold you on this concept. I am trusting you to make the right decision! I say "Go for It"!!

SECTION 11

Financial Considerations and Assistance

The Business Plan

For anyone not familiar with a business plan it is basically a *road map* for your business. I think you will agree, few people take a trip and don't know their destination. Granted, individuals retire and simply "hit the road" with no specific destination and no time line but their motivation is relaxation. They have already "paid their dues" and money is no longer an issue. You will be in this position before you know it but first, you have work to do and many exciting challenges to experience.

Okay, enough dreaming, back to the *road map* with a *destination.*

About now most everyone reading this guide is thinking to themselves: this guy is a little confused. Everybody knows the business plan is the very first and most important phase of any successful business but it looks like it's in the final section of this guide. So, what's the deal?

The deal is this: *I just wrote your business plan for you.* Actually I didn't write your business plan but I did give you every piece of information you will need to write an effective business plan. To be sure, you will not be including everything in this guide in your business plan. What you will be doing is picking and choosing the features you like and then summarizing. It's important to note, your business plan should not be much more than twenty pages so you will have to be quite selective with the information you include.

I have written many business plans but I am absolutely not the authority on writing a business plan. I will; however, give you some excellent resources for business plan assistance a bit later. Rest assured, they will be the "authority" on business plan writing so you will be in good hands. The best part: it's mostly, if not all, free.

Even though I said I was going to refer you to some excellent sources for composing and formulating a business plan, I would like to take a moment and give you a few quick pointers that I feel will prove to be quite beneficial with regards to your business plan.

I just mentioned the fact your business plan should not be very long. Twenty to twenty-five pages should be more than enough. Loan officers and investors are very busy people and they really don't have time to read a "novel". *They only want the facts and nothing but the facts!* Keep in mind, as far as business is concerned, individuals who lend money avoid getting emotional. It's strictly business. To be clear, these are good people with families and many good friends so they do have a "softer" side but when they are on the job that's not an option. So, choose your words carefully and avoid a lengthy business plan. It will be much more productive.

Another important feature of your business plan which is an absolute necessity is you must *always remind the lender as to how you will be generating the revenue to repay the loan.* Many business plans state what they plan on doing, they just don't spell out how, "What they are doing" will actually affect or improve their bottom line. Put yourself in the lender's position: they make money by lending money so they must be paid back in full and with interest in order for that scenario to work for them. Whether they lend you the money or not, it truly is not personal, they just want to know their money plus interest will be repaid to them in a timely manner. This way they will have funds to lend to another qualified applicant and make more money. As you can see, it's just business, so make it very clear in your business plan as to how, "What you do" will generate more revenue.

The Executive Summary

The executive summary is the most important feature of the business plan. When you see the word "summary" the assumption would be that it would appear at the end of the business plan. It actually appears close to the front of the business plan. The reason the executive summary appears close to the front of the business plan is so the loan officer or investor can easily locate and read it. The executive summary must be very brief and, in most cases, a page or less. The person reviewing your business plan will make the majority of their decision based on what they see in your executive summary. This summary could be a "make or break" for your business plan, not to mention the acquisition of the funds you may need to start your automotive business. As you may guess, this is where you really have to choose your words very carefully. They will be looking for keywords that will let them know you are a serious business person with direction, aspirations, determination, and goals. And, that you are extremely dedicated to your cause. So, a word to the wise, get your executive summary right the first time, your business funding could depend on it!

The Presentation

To be sure, I have not scratched the surface on all of the elements of writing a complete business plan. As mentioned, I am definitely not the authority on this subject: I am simply trying to stress some of the important considerations with regards to your business plan. These are tips I have gained over the years, and on the outside chance these tidbits of information don't happen to show up anywhere else, I think it is important you be aware of them. Now the presentation of your business plan.

The presentation of your business plan is as important as the business plan itself. Once your business plan is complete you must memorize each and every word so you can respond quickly and efficiently to questions you will be encountering during your interview. All of the information is in your business plan but the loan officer, or investor will want to check to make sure you know and understand what you wrote. For all they know, someone else could have written the entire business plan and you may have no idea as to the content.

There are many professional business plan writers who could very easily tell the lender what they want to hear just so you can get the funds to start your business. In this case, there is a chance you could get your funding but, since you would have no clue as to what you were doing, you would soon fall flat on your face. To summarize this point: "Business gone - Money Gone". This is not the point of doing a business plan or going into business so we definitely *do not* want this to happen.

Another very important aspect of the business plan presentation is your appearance and body language. It goes without saying, you should be neatly dressed but not overdressed. Your clothing and attire is very important but how you handle yourself will speak volumes as to your motivation and dedication to your new business venture.

Here is another suggestion: first and foremost, be at your appointment fifteen minutes early. Just so you know, in the business world: "If you are on time you are fifteen minutes late!". So, first order of business, be at your appointment fifteen minutes early.

Next, whether in the waiting area or in your appointment, always sit up straight and observe good posture. Keep in mind, this is business: it's not like you are at home watching TV, so never slouch or look like you are getting too comfortable. This will only make you look like a "slacker" and that will never impress anyone.

When you are in your appointment and you are asked a question, you should lean forward slightly, make and maintain eye contact and with a degree of assertiveness, respond to the questions with a clear and knowledgeable answer. Make sure you smile the entire time and do a quick "eyebrow twitch" each time you are trying to make a point. By "eyebrow twitch" I mean raise your eyebrows briefly and then return them to the normal position. ***I'm not kidding, this has a very positive psychological effect!!*** This and other facial expressions indicate you have energy and excitement so this always has a positive benefit.

Oh, by the way, no matter the outcome, always be polite and courteous from the time you arrive at your appointment until you leave. You never know, if the meeting did not have a positive outcome, the interviewer may reconsider his or her decision and your polite behavior could be a determining factor for this reconsideration. Always be polite: it will pay off.

Okay, I've managed to get this far and have given you only a few details as to the format and layout of an effective business plan. As I mentioned earlier, I am not the expert for business plan writing but, as promised, I'm going to tell you who is. If you recall, I also mentioned these services were free or at a very minimal cost.

Here we go: I am referring to the Small Business Administration (SBA) and the Service Corps of Retired Executives (SCORE). These are two of the most powerful business resources you could ever hope to have at your disposal. The SBA really wants you to acquire the funds to start your business venture and SCORE will do everything in their power to guide and direct you toward acquiring these funds. Between the two, you will be able to start and sustain your successful automotive business venture. SCORE works closely with the SBA but they are two totally different and unrelated entities. The SBA is a government agency while SCORE is a private, non-profit organization.

The Small Business Administration

Let's start with a brief overview on the SBA. In the interest of efficiency, I don't want to take up a lot of your time in this guide with regard to this topic. Their website is very complete and gives all of the details you will need. The following are some highlights you may not be familiar with.

Before I start I'm going to make the assumption most readers are not independently wealthy and obtaining a loan will be a necessity if you plan on going into business. Of course, you could possibly obtain financing through family or friends but that rarely has a happy ending. Unfortunately, "startup" businesses don't have a great track record and only the best and the strongest will survive. Fortunately, the auto repair business does well through "thick" or "thin" so that makes this a really good business to get in to. The important thing to remember is you will have this guide close at hand so you will not be alone in this business "*Adventure*".

In order to acquire a loan to start a business you will need to contribute a certain amount of your own cash or physical assets to show you are serious. In the business world this is known as ***"Skin in the Game".***

Without this "skin in the game" most lenders will not take you seriously. You can have all of the knowledge, ability and skill in the world but you will, most likely, not get a loan. They figure if you are not willing to risk any of your own assets then you could possibly walk away from your business because you have nothing to lose. At this point you may think you are out of luck but fortunately we have the SBA. You will still be required to contribute assets but, in most cases, not nearly as much. In return you will have to convince them you are up to the task of being a successful business owner and also have the ability to hang in there for the long haul.

The SBA mission statement is very detailed but in summary it states; "The SBA helps Americans start, build and grow businesses". The SBA was created in 1953 to provide and implement programs to achieve this goal. Their primary method of accomplishing this task is through delivering and guaranteeing loans, government contracts, business training, and other forms of assistance. Keep in mind, small business is the "engine" that keeps this nation moving forward so you can see the SBA has a very important and essential job.

Loans

For sure, most people assume the SBA only coordinates loans but, you can see, they do much more. Granted, loans may be their primary function but you need the total package in order to make these funds productive. Just so you know, loans are readily available to all qualified applicants. Your primary task is to convince the SBA you are a qualified applicant. The SBA really wants you to get the loan but they have to know you are the right person to receive these funds. There are lots of qualified individuals out there so you have to deliver the best plan and presentation and you will be set. Sounds easy enough, but it isn't. Not to worry though, you will have adequate assistance and coaching at little to no cost so you will enjoy success.

Entrepreneurial Development

This is the low to no cost education, information, technical assistance and training program offered by the SBA. They have multiple locations throughout the US so this service can be accessed at one of their local offices but can also be acquired online. They have several great features on their website but one of the best is their "Learning Center". Among other very important information, this is where you will learn the crucial details for your business plan. The SBA business plan format is considered the "standard of the industry" so that's the one I would recommend. Most, if not all banks, lending institutions and private investors respect this format. If you use this format, in most cases, you will only have to do one business plan if multiple presentations are required. The business plan section is only one of the many features available in their Learning Center so explore their entire website and you will be amazed at what you will learn.

Government Contracts

The SBA can also assist you with the coordination of government contracts. A little known fact is the government has a mandate for a statutory goal of awarding twenty three (23) percent of all government contracts to small business. About now you are thinking: "How would I ever be able to get a government contract if I'm specializing in auto repair?". As you may well know the government owns lots vehicles, many of which are located in your service area. It is a well-known fact, free enterprise is the most efficient and cost effective way of doing business. So, it would make a lot of sense that an independent auto repair facility perform the necessary maintenance on government owned vehicles. Depending on your service area it could be many or few vehicles but the important thing to remember is every little bit will add up to a substantial sum at the end of the year. This could be that little extra that will help you achieve your annual financial goals. I can tell you from experience I really appreciated the additional revenue it generated for me!

Advocacy - Voice for Small Business

Here is a feature of the SBA that I bet you were not aware of. I'm sure everyone has knowledge of the fact the SBA is in existence to benefit small business but I bet these same individuals don't realize the SBA reviews legislation and speaks out against any legislation that may have a negative impact on small business. For the record, that's a big deal! I've mentioned the importance of being a member of your automotive aftermarket association, Better Business Bureau and Chamber of Commerce because of the power of a group of people. Well, imagine the clout the SBA can exert in your favor. The beauty of this arrangement is, if you are a business owner, you are automatically a represented member of the SBA. I think you will agree, that's about as good as it can get.

Okay, I promised you I would not take up a lot of your time on this topic mainly because the SBA website is so very complete and easy to navigate that you are always better off going to the source for the most accurate information. I mainly wanted to enlighten you on some of the important benefits that are available to business owners, and to include those individuals, who have an interest in going into business.

I think you will agree with me that, based on the information I just reported to you, the SBA is quite an organization to have on your side. They are truly there to help.

Here is my very best advice with regard to the SBA. It will come as no surprise to you that, in the eyes of some people, government agencies and possibly even the SBA have, in the past, received some negative press. I will let you be the judge of that, but allow me to tell you what I would do in your position.

First and foremost, start off on the right foot. Upon the first and any subsequent visits, or other contact, with an SBA representative make sure you very briefly let them know how much you appreciate all of the services and benefits they offer and how helpful they have been. To be sure, you will be speaking the truth. Sincerity is the key in this situation. Keep in mind, you will gain more with that single "drop of honey" than you could ever get from "ten gallons of vinegar". You see, that representative is really going to appreciate your compliments and professional behavior and think to themselves: "We need more people like this in business". This could be the single factor which could tip the scales in your favor. I know it's worked for me. So, remember to always be respectful and nice to all SBA representatives: they are there to *Help* you!

As I have mentioned on several occasions, make certain you visit the SBA website for all of the important details concerning their organization. They will always be willing to help in any way possible to assist you in achieving your dream of owning your own auto repair business.

To summarize: Remember, an effective, well thought out business plan in conjunction with a professional presentation will do more to acquire your funds than just about anything else you can do. Once you get your funding it's time to deliver on your promises so get out there and show the world and the SBA what you are made of by creating and growing your successful auto repair business.

SCORE

As mentioned before, SCORE stands for the Service Corps of Retired Executives. I also mentioned the fact it is a private, non-profit organization. As the name indicates, this organization is made up primarily of retired business professionals. SCORE was created in 1964 to pair these seasoned, knowledgeable professionals with startup and all other individuals new to business. Business owners and potential business owners with little experience were desperately in need of guidance from these experienced, highly trained individuals. I forgot to mention these retired executives are most, if not all, volunteers. Their services are at little to no cost so you can't beat the price. Generally speaking, you shouldn't pay attention to free advice but this is truly the exception. Pay very close attention to what these volunteers have to say because they are always looking out for your best interest so make it a point to be "all ears" when they speak.

SCORE is not affiliated with the SBA but they have had an excellent working relationship for many years. This is another case where teamwork really pays off. SCORE has a complementary effect with the SBA. SCORE offers similar business training and educational opportunities as the SBA, with the primary difference in the two organizations being, SCORE does not lend money nor do they insure loans. To be sure, SCORE volunteers will do anything in their power to assist you with the acquisition of funds which will make that phase of the process somewhat easier.

Another benefit with SCORE is, it's always good to be exposed to differing points of view when in the process of making business decisions. I know there have been cases where I thought I "knew it all" and then an experienced, knowledgeable individual would make a suggestion and would put a totally different perspective on a situation. As a result, it completely changed the outcome, and for the better.

In addition to giving business advice and start up assistance they can also direct you with management, marketing, running and growing your business, technology, finance, money, mentoring, and workshops. One of their best programs is their "Business Plan Assist".

At the expense of sounding like a broken record, your business plan is your "roadmap" to success. Your business plan must be accurate and well thought out because, as with any roadmap, if it's not accurate you may be taking a wrong turn down a very "lonesome highway" and, I think you will agree, this must be avoided at all costs. Your SCORE volunteers will be your GPS system. Through their many years of experience, they will be able to give you turn by turn direction so you will not get lost. The good news: if you do happen to "veer" off of the road they will be there to get you back on course and headed to your destination.

Conclusion

This is by far the best information you will ever receive on starting and managing an auto repair facility. All of the information in this guide is the result of many hours, days, weeks, and years of trial and error, making big mistakes and trying new techniques. As I have said several times in this guide, I made all of the mistakes so you won't have to and, believe me, I made some whoppers! The good news is, you will be in a position to enjoy all of the benefits of my learning experience without having to worry about what to do when things go wrong.

One of the most important points I really want to get across is even if you have no automotive knowledge or skills, you can still be quite successful in the auto repair business. The most important characteristics you will need are good management and leadership skills and, then, following this guide will take care of the rest.

For all of the ladies who have ever considered owning an auto repair business but were sure it was an unattainable goal I say: *Not Anymore!* You can do it, and if I have anything to do with it you will succeed in the auto repair industry. I have said several times before, if I accomplish just one thing with this guide, I hope that one thing is to get more ladies involved in the auto repair business. You have the natural ability to manage, multi-task, communicate, and guide individuals to maximum efficiency. The auto repair industry desperately needs more individuals with these skills so come on down and step right up. I am certain the ladies are going to be the next generation of successful auto repair facility entrepreneurs.

Once again, for all those hardy souls who managed to make it to the end of this guide, you get the unique opportunity of viewing my contact information one more time. Lucky you: HaHa!!

My email is **alexdotson1@gmail.com**. I am available for email and/or on-site consultations so let me know what's on your mind. Waiting to hear from you!!

Thanks for reading my guide!

Alex Dotson

www.ingramcontent.com/pod-product-compliance
Lightning Source LLC
Chambersburg PA
CBHW041442210326
41599CB00004B/104

* 9 7 8 0 6 9 2 5 3 7 0 4 6 *